The Coaching Starter Kit:
Everything You Need to Know to Launch and Expand Your Coaching Practice

The Coaching Starter Kit:
Everything You Need to Know to Launch and Expand Your Coaching Practice

CoachVille.com

W.W. Norton & Company
New York • London

For information about permission to reproduce selections from this book, write to Permissions, W. W. Norton &
Company, Inc., 500 Fifth Avenue, New York, NY 10110

Production Manager: Anna Oler
Manufacturing by Haddon Craftsmen, Inc.

Library of Congress Cataloging-in-Publication Data

The coaching starter kit : everything you need to launch and expand your coaching practice / by CoachVille.com.
cm.
"A Norton professional book."
ISBN 0-393-70411-4 (pbk.)
1. Business consultants. 2. Consultants. I. CoachVille.com.

HD69.C6C555 2003
001'.068—dc21   2002044374

W. W. Norton & Company, Inc., 500 Fifth Avenue, New York, N.Y. 10110
www.wwnorton.com

W. W. Norton & Company Ltd., Castle House, 75/76 Wells St., London W1T 3QT

67890

Table of Contents

Alphabetical Listing of Forms

Note to the Reader

Mental health professionals who are eager to add a profitable and professionally fulfilling dimension to their practices are turning toward coaching in increasing numbers. Given that many coaching models incorporate and elaborate upon basic principles of psychology and psychotherapeutic practice, it isn't surprising that therapists have taken to the coaching profession so readily. According to a recent survey by *Psychotherapy Finances*, 20% of therapists now offer coaching in addition to psychotherapeutic services.

We hope that the book you are holding in your hands will offer you authoritative resources for opening a coaching practice as an adjunct to a psychotherapeutic practice, building a coaching practice from scratch, or fine-tuning a successful coaching venture. From practice design and attracting clients to session agendas, communication advice, and goal-oriented, issue-specific client worksheets, the material in this book will give you a panoply of coaching resources for you and your clients.

For readers who are currently licensed mental health professionals, we would like to offer *a note of caution*: Coaching is an evolving field and this pertains equally to the ethical and legal strictures guiding coaching practice. In general, coaching methods and customs do not follow the rules laid out by the American Psychological Association and the standards and practices of other professional mental health organizations in the United States. Some of the coaching strategies and procedures provided in the following pages—especially those pertaining to confidentiality, referrals, interstate phone sessions, and state-to-state billing—may not be appropriate for professionals who have a diversified practice. The forms provided here have *not* been adapted to conform to APA rules and regulations, and if you are a licensed mental health professional, you must adapt and interpret these forms accordingly to comply with pertinent professional standards. We urge readers with any questions concerning licensure and ethical codes to contact the appropriate professional organizations, including the International Association of Coaches (IAC).

Part 1
Coaching Practice Design 101

Chapter 1

What Is Coaching?

Coaching Explained

WHAT IS COACHING?

Coaching is quickly becoming one of the leading tools that successful people use to live extraordinary lives. Through weekly coaching sessions, clients identify what is most important to them and align their thoughts, words, and actions, accordingly. Coaches work with clients to identify what they want personally and professionally, and to support them in achieving a life that they really want and love. Having a life one loves starts with gaining clarity on values, enabling more meaningful choices and consistent action. Coaching offers a means for more balance, joy, intimacy, energy, financial abundance, focus, and action in every area of life.

A COACH WILL:

- Encourage clients to set goals that they truly want

- Ask clients to do more than they may have done on their own

- Help clients focus in order to produce results more quickly

- Provide clients with the tools, support, and structure to accomplish more

HOW IS COACHING DIFFERENT FROM THERAPY OR CONSULTING?

Unlike therapy, which goes into depth about various issues, usually dealing with the past, and consulting which generally results in giving the client answers, coaching is more action-oriented and focuses primarily on the present and future. Coaches enable clients to determine their own "answers" through the work done in the coaching partnership.

WHO WORKS WITH A COACH?

Entrepreneurs, business owners, professionals, and people in transition are some of the people who typically work with a coach. Regardless of their professional endeavors or place in life, clients have one thing in common: they are all successful, resourceful, and intelligent individuals who want to get even more out of their lives.

What professional athlete hasn't used a coach to win? Tiger Woods is already one of the best, and yet he understands the value of having someone work directly with him, pointing out things he can't see, encouraging and challenging him to achieve his greatest potential. Coaching is like having a personal trainer for your life!

The Coaching Process

There are 3 basic elements to the coaching process:

- Helping the client to discover and understand who they are

- Helping the client identify and clarify what they most want

- Helping the client to create and develop strategies to achieve their goals

We've found that coaching is so powerful because of the "who" element. Goals (what) and strategies (how) are terrific, but unless they are integrated with the person (who), they will take longer to accomplish, probably not be what the person really wants, and not result in the high levels of happiness and fulfillment that are possible.

The client and coach can start at any of the three portals (who, what, or how), and weave through all three, as needed, during the coaching process.

3-Step Coaching Model

From *The Coaching Starter Kit* by CoachVille.com, published by W.W. Norton & Company, Inc.

7

Basics of the Coaching Relationship

The trained coach is able to do so much with the client that both parties sometimes forget what they are there to accomplish together. Here is one view of the coaching relationship.

Who	The coach works with a client who wants to set a goal and who is willing to include another party in design, implementation, and success.
What	The client works with the coach to: 1. Become fully self-generative by being whole and well. 2. Take the time to think about the smart course of action. 3. Build a sustaining community for love, resources, and support.
Why	The coach is hired by a client to: 1. Accomplish something specific, personal, and/or professional. 2. Restore the client's soul and/or quality of life. 3. Contribute by discerning, developing, and sharing the client's gifts.

How	The coach coaches, using the following methods:
	 1. Sharing information
	   a. Drawing distinctions
	   b. Teaching principles
	   c. Offering perspective
	 2. Providing structure
	   a. Asking for a lot
	   b. Expecting the client's best
	   c. Being unconditionally constructive
	 3. Training
	   a. Being a model for the client
	   b. Walking the client through their growth
	   c. Giving specialized instruction

Where	The process of coaching occurs daily, regardless of how often the sessions are held:
	 1. Coaching conversations
	   a. Scheduled calls
	   b. Emergency calls
	   c. Success calls
	 2. Client support structures
	   a. Buddy system
	   b. Seminars led by coach
	   c. Social events hosted by coach
	 3. Client Homework
	   a. Promising to take action
	   b. Using client worksheets
	   c. Reading and studying

From *The Coaching Starter Kit* by CoachVille.com, published by W. W. Norton & Company, Inc.

9

Coaching Customs

Every profession has distinct ways of operating, and coaching is no different. Described below are the emerging customs of the professional coach. Not every coach follows every custom, but most coaches have experimented with these standards, procedures, policies, and ways of doing business.

WE WORK WEEKLY
Professional coaches work weekly, or more, with clients. We believe an ongoing, nurturing, and developing relationship works best for the client and coach and we encourage all clients to see us regularly. We offer three to four sessions per month, on average.

WE GIFT COACHING TO CLIENTS
Professional coaches work with up to five special clients who need the coach's services yet cannot pay full fare. We are in business, yet recognize that helping others is a way to show our gratitude.

THE CLIENTS' NEEDS COME FIRST
Professional coaches place people with the coach who can help that person the most. We don't keep clients for whom we cannot do a great job.

WE SHARE OUR COMMUNITY
Professional coaches are a resource for our clients and we do our best to put our clients in touch with people in our community for mutual benefit.

WE ARE PAID IN ADVANCE
Professional coaches are paid monthly, in advance, for individual coaching. We do not bill for each session.

WE HAVE OUR OWN COACH
Professional coaches always have a coach of their own. We believe that to be a developing coach, one must have a coach.

WE MAINTAIN A FULL PRACTICE
Professional coaches maintain a practice that is 50 percent greater than needed to pay business and personal expenses. We believe in maintaining a healthy reserve so that we can give straight, empowering advice.

COACHING, NOT THERAPY
Professional coaches work only with clients who can use us well. We are not therapists, parents, caretakers, or financial planners. We refer clients to the best available professionals for their psychological, health, and financial concerns. We help clients reach their goals.

WE ARE COMPLETELY CONFIDENTIAL
Professional coaches don't talk about their clients to anyone. We protect everything our clients tell us.

WE HAVE A NATIONAL PRACTICE
Many clients work with us on the telephone—from next door, across the state, and around the country. Generally, clients use the coach's 800 number.

WE KNOW MANY OTHER COACHES
We've gotten to know at least twenty other coaches for mutual support, cross referring, and professional development. Some coaches are members of the National Association of Professional Coaches, Inc.

WE ARE ON A PATH OF MASTERY
We understand that the field of coaching is evolving and we continually grow as well, both personally and professionally. Some of us are preparing to qualify for coaching certification.

WE HAVE MONEY IN THE BANK
Professional coaches maintain an emergency savings account of at least $10,000 so that no money concern gets in the way of our coaching of clients.

WE ARE AVAILABLE
We recognize the importance of the relationship we have with our clients and strive to keep ourselves emotionally, physically, mentally, and spiritually available so we can fully assist our clients.

WE PROTECT RELATIONSHIPS
Coaches complement the work of other professionals. We do not interfere with other professional relationships the client has. If a client is changing coaches, all parties are in full communication.

From *The Coaching Starter Kit* by CoachVille.com, published by W. W. Norton & Company, Inc.

Key Coaching Principles

1. **Synergy creates better results, much more easily**
   Coaching is synergistic through its collaborative nature between coach and client

2. **When people are fully heard and understood, they move forward instantly**
   Without this, people generally slow down—or even stop—in life

3. **Any situation can be optimized, turned around, or improved**
   And with a coach it can happen much more quickly

4. **Fewer problems occur when one has a strong personal foundation**
   Rising above the muck of life is job #1 in coaching

5. **Sometimes the client has the answer; sometimes the coach does**
   It really doesn't matter where the answers come from

6. **You can have a perfect life**
   Don't mock it until you've tried it

7. **We humans operate at 1 percent, or less, of our potential**
   Coaching increases this percentage

8. **Success is a basic human right**
   Success has nothing to do with deservedness, privilege, or background

9. **When the client properly defines success for him/herself, coaching accelerates**
   This knowledge naturally positions the client to be more successful with less effort

10. **Most people don't know what they truly want**
    A coach can help clients discover what they truly want—it's a fairly simple process

11. **What you put up with costs you dearly**
    Tolerations consume energy, resources, and the human spirit

12. **We are all Picassos-in-training**
    The world is waiting for everyone to discover, express, and share their creativity

From *The Coaching Starter Kit* by CoachVille.com, published by W. W. Norton & Company, Inc.
Form courtesy of and copyrighted by Thomas Leonard

100 Key Points About Coaching and the Coaching Process

This piece should come in handy for anyone preparing a brochure, presentation, or article on coaching.

1. WHY COACHING WORKS
What makes the process effective?
- Creative synergy/spark
- Emotional support/caring
- Intellectual challenge/evocation
- Outside influence/objectivity
- Interdevelopmentalism/exchange
- Complete confidentiality/safety
- Continual/immediate access
- Frequent interaction
- Type of questions asked/discussion

2. WHO HIRES A COACH
What are the primary markets?
- Entrepreneurs/business owners
- Consultants/trainers/coaches
- Psychologists/counselors
- CEOs/executives/HR
- Managers/supervisors
- Professionals (legal, financial, sales)
- Career changers/transitioners
- Creative types (writers/artists)
- Project managers
- Coaches from other disciplines

3. DRIVING DEMAND
Why is coaching becoming so popular?
- Entrepreneurism/self-employment
- Lifestyle preferences/dreams
- Self-determination/individualism
- Desire for self-expression
- Competitive advantage
- Increased loneliness and isolation in society

4. HOW TO FILL A PRACTICE
Your keys to success.
- Build a strong network
- Marketing letters
- Electronic newsletters
- Website/web presence
- Apprenticeship/skill sets
- Coach/client referrals
- Public relations/media
- Specialties/reputation
- TeleClasses/workshops
- Writing books/tapes/programs

5. KEY COACHING SKILLS
What types of skills work the best?
- Listening/hearing
- Clarifying/prioritizing
- Truth telling/integrating
- Messaging/languaging
- Gapping/distinctions
- Correcting/educating
- Challenging/evoking
- Directing/guiding
- Caring/supporting
- Training/demonstrating

6. COACHING FOCI/GOALS
Where do clients want to focus?
- Revenue/profitability
- Marketing/promotion

From *The Coaching Starter Kit* by CoachVille.com, published by W. W. Norton & Company, Inc.

15

- Communication/thinking skills
- Personal foundation/development
- Management/organizational skills
- Home/family life
- Integration/prioritization
- Personal lifestyle/freedom
- Financial independence
- Problem-solving/tolerations

7. BENEFITS OF COACHING

Why is coaching worthwhile?

- Clearer, more rewarding goals
- Faster results/advancement
- Clearer, sharper thinking
- More money/security
- Meaningful accomplishments
- Happier, more fulfilling life
- Higher profits and profitability
- Optimization of ideas
- Rapid personal evolution/development

8. FUTURE OF COACHING

What is on the horizon?

- Group/common-interest coaching
- On-call/as-needed coaching
- Web/e-mail/QuickCam coaching
- TeleClass coaching
- Specialty coaching/experts
- Niche coaching
- Hosting virtual communities
- International/global coaching
- Multiple-coach/single-client coaching
- Annual fee/coach-training packages

9. CLIENT PRIORITIES

What will clients want more of?

- Willingness/optimism
- Openness/flexibility
- Creativity/experimentation
- Commitment/dedication
- Communication/relating
- Effectiveness/efficiency
- Integrity/responsibility
- Integration/balance
- Organization/space
- Love/energy

10. SOURCE OF COACHING

Where do coaching principles come from?

- Business/management theories
- The sciences/nature/life
- Common sense/proven wisdom
- Education/teaching skills
- Sports and teamwork skills
- Awareness/Eastern philosophy
- Parenting/community skills
- Communication/relating skills
- Motivation/inspiration techniques
- Psychology/self-help practices

From *The Coaching Starter Kit* by CoachVille.com, published by W. W. Norton & Company, Inc.

Should You Be a Coach?

Coaching is not for everyone, but it may be for you. Coaching is becoming a popular profession. Business consultants, therapists, teachers, entrepreneurs, trainers, and other advisors find the quality of work and clientele appealing enough to invest in the training and required time. Allow about five years to become an established coach, but a number of entrants earn six figures by the end of their third or fourth year, so they must be doing something right! Take this little quiz to see if coaching is the right profession for you. (If not, perhaps you will enjoy it as a hobby or opportunity to contribute to others.)

Check the box which most applies. Then, score yourself using the key at the end of the test.

YES	UMM	NO	STATEMENT
❑	❑	❑	I truly enjoy people just as they are.
❑	❑	❑	I'm not afraid of anybody.
❑	❑	❑	People have been coming to me for counsel for a long time.
❑	❑	❑	I love to help and am willing to relearn how to do it right.
❑	❑	❑	I don't mind the ups and downs of being self-employed.
❑	❑	❑	I am truly fine just the way I am, but I like to grow, too.
❑	❑	❑	As far as I am concerned, people do not need fixing.
❑	❑	❑	I am on a rewarding path of self-awareness.
❑	❑	❑	I have a good grasp of how life can work effortlessly.
❑	❑	❑	People consistently listen and respond to me.
❑	❑	❑	I can easily charge money for my coaching.
❑	❑	❑	I could tell people to work with me. I don't mind selling my expertise.
❑	❑	❑	I am well-connected with a strong network to attract clients.
❑	❑	❑	I'll do whatever it takes to get a full practice in one year.
❑	❑	❑	I can invest $1,000-$5,000 in the first year for training and expenses.
			Totals for *Yes, Umm*, and *No* boxes
x 3	x 1		
			Points for *Yes* and *Umm* answers (no points for *No* answers)
			Total of *Yes* and *Umm* points

SCORING KEY

Yes   3 pts

Umm   1 pt

No   0 pt

Minimum score to seriously consider becoming a professional coach is 30 points (max is 45).

7 Benefits of Being a Professional Coach

BENEFIT #1

You double your rate of personal development.

One of the fastest ways for a person to grow is to coach others. When you are accountable for results, share distinctions, and give advice, you learn. In fact, you'll learn 80 percent of what you need to know directly from your clients. A mentor coach or coach training program does give you the critical 20 percent, but you should consider your clients as your real trainers. You spend a lot of time with them and learn much about yourself in the process.

BENEFIT #2

You can make an extraordinary living.

Coaches earn between $25,000 and $200,000 per year. A few earn even more.

Hourly fees range from $25 to $225. It takes a lot of training and experience to earn the higher numbers. You can start making that kind of money if you are extraordinary, attract entrepreneurial or corporate clients, and if coaching is the right profession for you.

If $50,000 a year is the right income for you, that can take between one and three years to reach.

The point is, coaching can be a well-paying profession with proper training, having the gift of coaching, and being part of a strong network.

BENEFIT #3

You build lasting, empowering relationships.

People who coach and clients who want to be coached are special people because they understand and value the power of synergy and partnership. They are at a place in life where being a Lone Ranger is not effective and not fun.

There is nothing wrong or unethical with having a client be your friend, assuming both of you are up to it. Clients become your partners in life, because they are contributing to you just as you are contributing to them. (Be careful, though. Some clients need all the focus on them initially, particularly if they are going through a transition or challenging time. Be selective.)

Notice that new clients are usually preoccupied with themselves and their issues. If a friendship occurs, it will develop over time.

BENEFIT #4

You become a master of life.

A full-time coach is on a path of development that leads to what we call mastery. If you've learned the distinctions of coaching, managed a full practice for several years, and taken care of your own life accordingly, chances are you'll be extraordinary.

BENEFIT #5

You are well-positioned for the next opportunity.

Some coaches are built to coach for a lifetime. Others love the profession, but will move on after four or five years. The profession is full of opportunities—many of which are revealed through time.

The skills you learn, the growth you experience, and a great group of people (colleagues, clients, and friends) set you up to notice, participate in, and benefit from opportunities such as:

- going into business with a client (be careful)
- getting involved in national issues
- writing and speaking, and more

BENEFIT #6

You get to give your gift.

We all have a special gift—a set of skills, a unique ability, a natural passion. Most coaches have a strong desire to empower others and contribute to them. Being a professional coach gives you "license" to do just that, full-time, while you make a living. Wow! What could be better?

BENEFIT #7

You will be appreciated.

Coaching another person is a contribution—and many clients will love you for it. Coaches shouldn't coach to get love, but you will get it. So, enjoy!

From *The Coaching Starter Kit* by CoachVille.com, published by W. W. Norton & Company, Inc.
Form courtesy of and copyrighted by Thomas Leonard

Chapter 2

Getting Started

STEP #1

Discover why you really want to be a coach, and be turned on about it.

Throughout my teen years, I knew I wanted to be a physician, so much did I want to help people. Finally, I wised up in 1988 and chose coaching as my profession.

People who coach well are those who love people and want the most for them. A coach usually has a knack for recognizing the strengths and assets of another.

Given this ability, the coach can give good advice, listen between the words, and educate the client to take full advantage of opportunities. This kind of consulting turns the coach on in a healthy, fulfilling way.

STEP #2

Get in a good space, personally. Your coaching can only be as good as your life is.

Coaching others is a responsibility; clients entrust themselves, their visions, and their goals with you. You must be healthy, able, and balanced before you enter the coaching profession.

You should be in touch with yourself, clear of any past traumas or critical therapy issues, and be in excellent health, free from addictions or attachments.

In other words, no smoking, no alcohol, drug, or eating abuses, and no caffeine. You can't be addicted or attached and coach well.

STEP #3

Hire a mentor coach; learn from an expert.

People who attempt to develop a coaching practice by themselves are rarely successful. Why?

Because coaching is both an art and a technology, and requires a mentoring structure to ensure the proper balance.

As a beginner or intermediate-level coach you will be faced with client situations that will shock, scare, and/or stump you. Your mentor coach has been there

before and will assist you to handle the situation professionally.

Plan to spend between $3,000 and $10,000 per year in your own coaching and training during your first three years in business. This investment pays off fully and quickly, so don't skimp. Coaching calls for an investment in yourself and your skills.

STEP #4

Set a $100,000 per year earnings goal with an action plan.

A professional, full-time coach should earn $100,000 within three to five years of being mentored and trained. $100,000 would mean forty hours a week of coaching at $50 per hour, or half-time at $100 per hour. To get to this level requires several things:

- Scheduled, bite-sized goals
- A willingness to work
- A financial reserve

Most coaches transition from a previous career, such as consulting or another profession. This transition is best achieved by designing an ultra-conservative plan, assuming a slow start to filling one's practice, and having a steady stream of income from a career or investment source.

A written plan makes the transition to full-time coaching easier and safer.

STEP #5

Treat coaching as a business, not just as a calling.

The most successful coaches have business clients, not personal ones. Entrepreneurs, self-employers, professionals, managers, and investors are those most likely to pay you well.

Those seeking personal growth, spirituality, and help with crises can be viable clients, but don't always have the budget to pay you $150 per hour or $10,000 per year.

From *The Coaching Starter Kit* by CoachVille.com, published by W. W. Norton & Company, Inc.
Form courtesy of and copyrighted by Thomas Leonard

23

Coaching is a business. You charge a fee for your time; the client should expect enough results to continue the relationship.

Send out bills monthly and insist on timely payment.

Make a substantial profit yourself; you'll attract more clients willing to pay more.

STEP #6

Attract clients who are ready now for what you have to offer.

A coach usually attracts clients who are either a step behind or a step ahead of you in your own life. Anything more and you're in over your head; anything less and you're bored.

You want to ask for and attract the clients who appreciate where you are in life and where you've come from. It inspires most clients to learn that you have courage, strength, and determination.

Some coaches coming into the field are concerned about their credentials. Must I have a degree? Should I wait to coach until I have more experience? Who would hire me?

I have plenty of credentials, but rarely mention them to prospective clients. Rather, my successful clients are my credentials. If a prospective client can't "get" that, they probably aren't ready for a coach. Know your current skills and natural abilities and offer these to people you meet.

You don't have to be an expert in every area of coaching.

STEP #7

Deliver 120 percent and your practice will fill simply from referrals.

The most-asked question from prospective coaches is, "How will I get my clients?"

Deliver 120 percent of what the client expects and your practice will fill itself.

And how does one deliver 120 percent?

Here are few ways:

- Keep client expectations low
- Be unconditionally constructive
- Ask clients to do more
- Don't accept excuses
- Expect a lot from them

Clients want you to be straight, loving, and relentless.

STEP #8

Know what you must know, then master it.

After you have selected your niche or specialty, design a plan to learn and master everything about that area.

If your focus is on entrepreneurs, read, study, practice, and interview. If turn-around situations interest you, develop a model for that. If life transition work gets you up in the morning, learn the dynamics of people and change.

Whatever the specialty, don't just learn it, master it!

STEP #9

Upgrade your practice. Charge more than you think you are worth.

Double your fees after a year of being in full-time practice, with the advice of your mentor coach.

You'll attract people who would not pay you $75 per hour, but will pay you $100 per hour.

Notice that the step is to charge more than you think you're worth; not more than you are worth. If you do, you will lose clients or it will come back to bite you.

Charge what you're worth, and train to be worth much, much more.

STEP #10

Mentor a novice coach. Pass on the gift of coaching.

Now it is your turn to teach others. Cherish the privilege. Mentoring another coach brings you to the next level.

Practice Design

Please complete each sentence in the space provided.

I WORK WITH PEOPLE WHO

Are _____

Want_____

Can _____

I SPECIALIZE IN THE FOLLOWING AREAS OF COACHING

❑ _____

❑ _____

❑ _____

SPECIAL FEATURES OF MY COACHING ARE

❑ _____

❑ _____

❑ _____

SPECIFIC BENEFITS OF MY COACHING TO CLIENTS ARE

❑ _____

❑ _____

❑ _____

BASIC MESSAGE I SHARE WITH CLIENTS IS

❑ _____

❑ _____

❑ _____

WHAT MAKES MY COACHING IRRESISTIBLE IS

❑ _____

❑ _____

❑ _____

5 SERVICE UPGRADES I OFFER THAT MOST CONSULTANTS DO NOT ARE

❑ _____

❑ _____

❑ _____

SUPER SIX REFERRAL SOURCES

❑ _____ has agreed to send me _____ clients

❑ _____ has agreed to send me _____ clients

❑ _____ has agreed to send me _____ clients

❑ _____ has agreed to send me _____ clients

❑ _____ has agreed to send me _____ clients

❑ _____ has agreed to send me _____ clients

FINANCIAL SUCCESS

I charge $ _____ per month and/or $ _____ per hour

My practice is full with _____ clients @ an average of $ _____ /mo = $ _____ month

MY CLIENTS COME VIA

1. _____

_____

2. _____

_____

3. _____

_____

I work an average of _____ hours per week, as follows _____.

I spend _____ hours per week marketing myself, which is _____ % of my billing hours.

My entire business expenses are $ _____ per month which is _____ % of my income.

ULTIMATELY, MY PRACTICE LOOKS LIKE THIS

Monthly revenue $ _____

Number of clients   _____

Weekly billed hours   _____

Hourly rate $ _____

From *The Coaching Starter Kit* by CoachVille.com, published by W.W. Norton & Company, Inc.

ATTRACTING CLIENTS
Top 5 Questions to Ask a Potential Client

1. What is the biggest change you would like to make in your life, assuming you had enough support to do it right?

_____

_____

_____

_____

2. If you hired me as your coach, what is the first thing we would work on together?

_____

_____

_____

_____

3. What's the hesitation about getting started?

_____

_____

_____

_____

4. How do you define success for yourself at this stage of your life?

_____

_____

_____

_____

5. What are the three biggest challenges you are facing right now?

_____

_____

_____

_____

From *The Coaching Starter Kit* by CoachVille.com, published by W. W. Norton & Company, Inc.
Form courtesy of and copyrighted by Thomas Leonard

The Importance of Sales Skills

1. **There is an important distinction between knowing how to coach and knowing how to market/sell your service**

   If you do not master the latter, even if you believe you are a great coach, you will starve. The coaches who have been most successful have this marketing/sales piece in their background.

2. **You need to let go of your negative associations with the word "sales"**

   Many coaches are fearful about sales and selling—that they will come across as a used car salesperson who wants to talk you into buying a car that does not run properly. The truth is, nothing happens until there is a sale. You can call it attraction, call it enrollment, but nothing happens until someone agrees to do business with you and pay for your service.

3. **Giving away free coaching sessions is for amateurs**

   Other professionals do not give away their services for free—why should a coach? For example, you wouldn't want to go to a doctor who says, "Let me treat you free for a month, then I know you will want to be my patient!" would you? Likewise, lawyers do not offer free legal services in hopes that you will retain them—why should you?

4. **The master sales skill is learning how to conduct a professional consultative interview to help a prospect discover why he/she needs your service**

   Doctors, lawyers, CPAs, and other professionals offer free consultations (using a systematic series of questions) to help their prospects come to their own conclusion about whether or not they need help. This is a far cry from the high-pressure sales tactics of amateur salespeople in all professions.

5. **Don't you believe you are a good coach?**

   Don't you believe you have something great to offer people through coaching? Then why would you want to rob someone of the opportunity to become your client? It is not a capital crime, but there ought to be a law against a coach who improperly engages a good prospective client without helping that person make a smart decision about becoming his/her client. Do not assume that the potential clients do not need you to help them make this very important choice to hire you. Selling skills help you help them buy your professional service.

From *The Coaching Starter Kit* by CoachVille.com, published by W. W. Norton & Company, Inc.
Form courtesy of and copyrighted by Jim Rohrbach, Success SkillsCoach

Selling Questions for the Potential Client

- What are 3 challenges you are facing right now?
- What is the financial opportunity you are missing out on because you are too busy dealing with problems?
- What outcome would make coaching worthwhile?
- What can I say that would interest you in having your own coach?
- What's the most exciting thing about your job?
- What do you feel passionate about? What gets you out of bed in the morning?
- What do you have some of, that you'd like a lot more of?
- What is it about coaching that sounds most interesting?
- How do you think you would benefit from partnering with a coach?
- What would be different if you worked with a coach?
- If you wanted to make more of an impact on your job, what are 2 or 3 things you would do differently?
- There's so much more I'd like to learn about you and what you're doing—and to tell you more about what I do. Are you available to speak sometime?
- Would you be interested in knowing the kind of people I coach?
- Would you like to know what a coach does?
- Is there something you would like some help with right now?
- Would you be interested in my coaching you in one of the areas you have mentioned to me?
- Would having some support with that be helpful? May I be so bold as to ask when you would like to start?
- If you want to improve _____, why not begin by hiring me?
- How's your foundation—your personal foundation?
- How are you solving the problems or concerns in your life?
- If there were a perfect solution, what would it be?
- Have you set your life up to take full advantage of that opportunity?
- How ready are you reaching your goals?
- Have you worked with a coach before?
- Who's around to keep you stretching the vision you have for your life?
- Have you ever considered the possibility of having a perfect life?
- What do I need to say so that you might give coaching a try?
- What do you really want in your personal life that you've never told anyone?
- Why wait for that? Why not start working on that right now?
- What is the gift or skill you want to use more often?

From *The Coaching Starter Kit* by CoachVille.com, published by W. W. Norton & Company, Inc.
Contributors: Thomas J. Leonard, Sandy Vilas, Marlene Elliott

- Would you let me help you with that problem?

- What consumes your time that isn't making you any money?

- What are you putting up with (tolerating)?

- Are you living your life or just working for a lifestyle?

- What is motivating you at this point in your life?

- What's something that you really, really want?

- Where do you hold yourself back?

- On a scale of 1 to 10, with 10 being highest, where, honestly, would you rate your personal quality of life right now?

- What are you doing that makes no sense at all?

- If you did hire a coach, where would you like to start your coaching work?

- How much would it be worth to you to solve your problems?

- What's in the way of your having a perfect life?

- Have you ever considered having a coach of your own?

- What are the 3 changes you would make in your life that would significantly improve it within a week?

- If you could have any type, or amount, of support with that, what would it include?

- What can't you do for yourself that perhaps a partner like a coach could help you do?

- Am I the first professional coach you've met?

- May I tell you how I work?

- What questions do you have about coaching?

- May I tell you a little bit about a client I've worked with who was facing something similar?

- How can I help?

- What would be the perfect solution for that?

- What are the strategies you are considering using to accomplish that most quickly?

- Do you have everything you want in your personal life?

- Would it help to talk to a coach about that?

- Who coaches you?

- How long has that been the case?

- When would you like to start working together?

- Is that problem solvable?

- If not now, when?

- Would you like a referral to someone whom I trust?

From *The Coaching Starter Kit* by CoachVille.com, published by W. W. Norton & Company, Inc.
Contributors: Thomas J. Leonard, Sandy Vilas, Marlene Elliott

A Consultative Approach to Enrolling New Clients

CONCEPT	SUGGESTED WORDS/TACTICS
Introduction with Benefit	Hi! I am a coach and my name is _____. I help people like you to ...
Positioning	I am really a consultant rather than a salesperson. In that regard, I am not here to sell you anything. My biggest fear is that I will talk you into something you really do not need.
Up Front Contract (Ground Rule Commitment)	If I could get fifteen or twenty minutes of your time to ask you a few questions, we can make a decision together—if it makes sense for us to do something further, or not. Does that sound fair?
Interview	Proceed with a consultative interview/examination for your product/service, using a series of questions to determine the probability of your prospect becoming a client. 1. Gap between where they are now versus where they could be with your product/service 2. Budget/Ability to pay 3. Decision-making process/timeframe 4. Conditions of satisfaction (Your skillful questioning will be all you need to determine if you and your prospect are truly a good fit.)
Directive Close Steps	If there is a good fit, tell the prospect the exact steps you and he/she will go through to become an active client. (If this sounds interesting to you, the way it works is _____.) Then, be quiet! The prospect will either agree to proceed or will present an objection. If there is an objection, go back to the interview to determine the prospects' concerns. Redefine them in terms of the conditions of satisfaction. Then, restate the step for becoming a client. (Note: If another meeting is required, you must set a firm appointment date, time, and agenda—even if by telephone.)

From *The Coaching Starter Kit* by CoachVille.com, published by W.W. Norton & Company, Inc.
Form courtesy of and copyrighted by Jim Rohrbach, Success Skills Coach

Top 5 Features of the Coaching Service

Like any other professional service, coaching has features and benefits. Here are some of the easiest-to-sell personal features of coaching.

1. **Your presence and dedication**

   Your being there is worth at least 50 percent of your fee, and the more sophisticated your client, the higher the percentage, in their eyes. Finding a coach who is there with them is a challenge for anyone looking for professional services.

   What is "there"? Caring, listening, focusing on, being honest with, standing in the shoes of, and challenging the client; thinking of the client between sessions, coming up with ideas for the client on your own without prompting, etc.

   Selling this feature: "One of the things you will get by working with me is that I am there— intellectually, emotionally, and spiritually. You will feel this—it's palpable. Especially between our calls, when the going gets rough, you can always call me!"

2. **Your set of related experiences and knowledge**

   We all have experiences and knowledge, but are you sharing the specifics of these so that the potential client has reason to believe in you?

   Bad Form: "I have been coaching for 25 years." (vague, quantity-vs-quality oriented)

   Good Form: "Based on what you have said, I have worked with three clients with similar opportunities. Would you be interested in hearing how they leveraged these similar opportunities?"

   Moral of the story: Show—don't tell.

3. **A creative and collaborative environment**

   The best clients want someone who can help them come up with clever strategies, solutions, and approaches to their goals and problems. It is important to educate the potential client that this creative environment is part of what you offer as a coach.

   Here is a way to weave this into a conversation with a potential client:

   "How creative are you going to have to be in order to solve that problem?"

   "Part of what you will be getting from a coach is a fresh, but experienced, set of eyes and ears. That contributes to the creative exchange between us. Creativity and collaboration are the best solutions to most problems. Either we will find the solution together, or we will create the solution, together."

From *The Coaching Starter Kit* by CoachVille.com, published by W. W. Norton & Company, Inc.

Form courtesy of and copyrighted by Thomas Leonard

35

4. **The basic structure of the coaching relationship/service**

   It's one of life's truisms: "With the perfect amount of support and structure, a person can do just about anything."

   Make sure that the client understands this. Here's one way to educate the client about this by asking a question:

   "If you knew that you had all the professional support and structure that you needed to perform at your best, what's the goal you would set for yourself?"

5. **Your professional network**

   When the client hires you, they are also getting access to the experts and specialists in your professional network. This saves your client a lot of searching because you have essentially prescreened these experts.

   Here are two examples of ways to weave into the conversation the fact that you have a valuable network:

   - "Will you be wanting someone to set up an e-commerce solution for you in the next six months? If so, I have got just the person."

   - "Within a couple months of our working together, you may want to include a focus on personal fitness and I can set you up with a gifted nutritionist who takes the mystery out of the process."

   Having a professional network adds significantly to your credibility and professionalism.

From *The Coaching Starter Kit* by CoachVille.com, published by W. W. Norton & Company, Inc.
Form courtesy of and copyrighted by Thomas Leonard

Top 5 Ways to Convert Your Website Visitors into Paying Clients

Now that you have got 10, 100, or 1,000 visitors coming to your coaching website each week, how do you convert them into clients? Here are five strategies that work very, very well.

1. **Show the visitor they have landed at the perfect website for what they need right now**

   Very few visitors to your website need to learn about coaching. What they need is someone who can help them solve their problem/dilemma or help them make the most of an opportunity.

   Suggestion: Don't simply list testimonials about how great a coach you are, rather, describe 10-25 specific situations in which you do your best work for your clients. This helps the visitor to see themselves and their situation as opposed to just seeing you at your website.

2. **Provide the option for the visitor to sign up for your e-zine on your home page**

   Most potential clients will only visit your site once, so it's key to get their e-mail address so that you can market to them later—and forever, if they let you. How many visitors are you losing as clients because you have no way to keep in touch with them?

   Suggestion: Remember, most clients take time to warm up to you, and your weekly or monthly newsletter or e-zine is the most efficient way to let them do this. Start an e-zine today. Every e-mail is worth about $10 to $100 to you if you market your services well.

3. **Offer an immediate take-away resource with your name on it**

   Post some top 10 lists, how-to guides, a free e-book, problem-solving steps, or life or business planning forms. These all act as brochures and remind the visitor who you are.

   Suggestion: Remember, visitors to your coaching website are probably surfing around many websites. Give them material to read and take with them on their journey.

4. **Make a direct offer to help the visitor in any way that you can**

   Most visitors to your website are looking for something. They may know—or they may not know— exactly who or what they are looking for in terms of a coach. Make it quite clear that you can either help them directly or refer them to someone who can.

   Suggestion: Position yourself as a well-connected resource, and make your e-mail address and telephone number prominent on every page. Educate the visitor on how you can help him/her decide whether to become a client or not, and/or offer a free session with no obligation.

5. **Invest in a highly credible-looking website**

   Typically, websites for coaches run between $1,000 and $10,000 to design, develop, and write. Also, a client is generally worth between $3,000 and $25,000 over their customer life cycle.

   Suggestion: Do the math, then contract with a talented designer who understands how to convert visitors into clients, and has the graphic flair to make your site credible, appealing, easy to use, and the best possible calling card for you. The biggest mistake coaches make regarding their websites is not having their site professionally designed. All the marketing in the world will not convince visitors to hire you if your site does not engender trust and credibility.

From *The Coaching Starter Kit* by CoachVille.com, published by W. W. Norton & Company, Inc.
Form courtesy of and copyrighted by Thomas Leonard

Top 5 Objections Raised by Potential Clients

Most potential clients want to work with a coach. But, as potential clients, they often have objections to starting. Usually these objections are not real but perceived. So, your job is to help them get over these, without being too pushy. Remember, your prospective clients do want to work with you; they are simply afraid, hesitant, or unclear of the focus. You can help them make a great buying decision.

1. **Objection: "I don't have time work with a coach."**

   Possible responses:

   - "Why are you that busy?"
   - "And how healthy is the stress in your busy schedule?"
   - "Perfect! I only work with clients who are way too busy to work with me."
   - "Perfect! Let's spend 30 days getting you ahead of your busy schedule."

2. **Objection: "I can't afford the coaching fee."**

   Possible responses:

   - "We all have the money we need for what we really want. What's the goal you'd set for yourself that you really want?"
   - "Are you living that close to the financial edge?"
   - "Let's first start working on getting you a financial reserve!"
   - "No problem. Let me discount it for you for the first 90 days. How much do you feel is both fair and affordable for you, to get started."

3. **Objection: I'm not sure what I would work on with a coach."**

   Possible responses:

   - "Yes, that's pretty typical. We usually spend a couple of sessions to sort out the various priorities you have. That itself is coaching."
   - "What are the 3 biggest challenges you are facing right now?"
   - "What is draining/zapping your energy most?"
   - "What is the opportunity that's going to pass you by if you don't act on it?"

4. **Objection: "I'm not sure that a coach can help."**

   Possible responses:

   - "Really. Why?"
   - "Is the problem overwhelming?"
   - "Would this be your first time working with a coach?"
   - "With what part don't you think a coach could help?"

5. **Objection: "I've already got a mentor."**

   Possible responses:

   - "What aren't you working on with him/her that you would still like some strategic support with?"
   - "Do you have a personal goal or problem that would benefit from immediate, dedicated attention?"
   - "Wonderful! What sort of things do you two focus on?" (then, listen for what else you could offer . . .)

From *The Coaching Starter Kit* by CoachVille.com, published by W. W. Norton & Company, Inc.
Form courtesy of and copyrighted by Thomas Leonard

39

New Client Checklist

Check each box as you complete each step.

Client _____

BEFORE ACCEPTING A CLIENT

- ❏ Do I really want to work with this person?
- ❏ What are the three things I know I can do for them?
- ❏ Will they stick around for at least 6 months?
- ❏ Can I learn a lot from this relationship?
- ❏ Will this person add to my practice and reputation?
- ❏ Is this person going to be able to pay the coaching fee, and on time?
- ❏ Is this person ready for a coach, or do they need someone/something else?

AFTER ACCEPTANCE, BEFORE THE FIRST SESSION

- ❏ Schedule first call or appointment.
- ❏ Find out what the person wants to work on most.
- ❏ Get a minimum three-month agreement.
- ❏ Get a check for the first month's coaching.
- ❏ Send paperwork/assessments to complete prior to the first session.
- ❏ Review the ground rules, agreements, and terms of the relationship.
- ❏ Double-check to make sure the client is ready and right for this.

DURING THE FIRST SESSION

- ❏ Welcome the client.
- ❏ Design up to three goals or projects to work on for ninety days.
- ❏ Get all of the assessment scores.
- ❏ Discern where on the path of development the person is.
- ❏ Discern the current obstacles to success.
- ❏ Tell the client what to do during the session.
- ❏ Give the client three pieces of homework.
- ❏ Schedule next/subsequent sessions.

Client Lead Form

Name _____ Occupation _____

Address _____

City _____ State _____ Zip _____

Day Phone _____ Evening Phone _____

Fax _____ Call Back Date _____

SOURCE

Referral from _____

Workshop/Speech _____

INTEREST LEVEL

❑ Immediate start

❑ Very interested

❑ Interested

❑ Curious

ACTION TAKEN

❑ Scheduled meeting

❑ Sent materials

❑ Called, left message

❑ Discussed coaching

❑ _____

WAITING FOR

❑ Decision

❑ Timing

❑ _____

CONSIDERATIONS

❑ Time

❑ Money

❑ Timing

❑ Value

❑ Partner: Okay

❑ _____

FOCUS AREAS

❑ Money

❑ Work

❑ Relationship

❑ Problem-solving

❑ Change

❑ Health

❑ Balance

❑ _____

FOR MY CLIENT, I WANT

_____

_____

_____

_____

_____

NOTES

_____

_____

_____

_____

_____

_____

_____

_____

_____

Client Retention Checklist

Clients do leave, but use this list and they'll stick around twice as long.

ACTION

❏ Send birthday and holiday cards.

❏ Never withhold anything from your client. Always share with them your concerns about them, a problem they are causing you, a fear you have about them. Don't censor or try to phrase it "right."

❏ Tell your client what you want for them as often as you can.

❏ Give flowers, a gift for their desktop, something special whenever they have a big win or need a lift.

❏ Always make the client pay by the beginning of the month. Accept nothing else.

❏ Have a full practice and a waiting list.

❏ Have a written agreement of at least three months.

❏ Always underpromise. Never even hint that you can produce miracles.

❏ Don't dwell on the client's (or your own) personality or issues—keep the focus on actions, distinctions, and coaching.

❏ Speak with your client at least once a week between scheduled calls.

❏ Invite your client to social events, like dinner and special luncheons. Make it social, but talk only about them, not yourself.

❏ Schedule special workshops for clients and their friends only.

❏ Don't push your clients for referrals—let them know you appreciate the referrals, but don't bug.

❏ Send out a quarterly letter or newsletter to keep your clients abreast of all that you are doing.

❏ Get the client focused on a very big and exciting goal or project. Challenge them, don't coddle.

❏ Don't put up with anything—missed calls, late to a call, complaining.

From *The Coaching Starter Kit* by CoachVille.com, published by W. W. Norton & Company, Inc.
Form courtesy of and copyrighted by Pavla Michaela Polcarova, CPR Coaching Services

Sixty Referrals

	CLIENT	REFERRAL #1	REFERRAL #2	REFERRAL #3
1.				
2.				
3.				
4.				
5.				
6.				
7.				
8.				
9.				
10.				
11.				
12.				
13.				
14.				
15.				
16.				
17.				
18.				
19.				
20.				

From *The Coaching Starter Kit* by CoachVille.com, published by W.W. Norton & Company, Inc.

47

CLIENT WELCOME MATERIALS
Welcome, Thank You, and Congratulations!

Thank you for your decision to start your coaching program with me. I appreciate your business and I would like you to read this letter before our first session so that you can get the absolute best out of your coaching experience. In this letter, I take you through what you can expect of yourself, of me, and of the coaching process in general.

Also, congratulations! I am proud to say that clients who have followed my guidance have been getting great results and great resolve towards ever-increasing levels of success and happiness in their lives. You should expect the same, so I congratulate you on taking a big step toward investing in the most valuable asset you will ever have—you!

WHAT YOU MAY EXPECT BEFORE OUR FIRST SESSION

The coaching experience begins the moment you make a commitment to your first session. Many clients report one or more of the following experiences prior to this session: curiosity, doubts, excitement, unexpected negative and/or high emotions, or uncertainty about the whole idea of coaching. Should similar feelings arise in you, please understand that all of these symptoms are completely normal and expected. In fact, they are often a sign that you are ready to make major positive shifts, and that your surroundings and your body are preparing for these shifts to take place.

If you wish, take notes of feelings and events as they surface and have them ready for our first session. If you are having doubts about the process, remember that you get a risk-free 30-day trial period to find out for yourself if the process is going to make the kind of difference in your life that I promised. If you have specific questions to ask about any part of the process, please call me before we get together to make sure that you get your questions answered during the first session.

WHAT YOU CAN EXPECT OF ME DURING OUR COACHING RELATIONSHIP

- **Confidentiality**   All of our interactions (conversations, e-mail, faxes, etc.) will remain strictly confidential, meaning that I will not share any information provided by you with anyone without your express consent. The exception to this will be that, from time to time, I may use a situation from your coaching experience as an analogy in another client's session, or in a public setting such as a newsletter or a seminar. In this case, I will not use your name and will refer to the situation in such a way that you will not be identifiable to others.

- **Availability**   You may contact me outside of our scheduled sessions if you would prefer not to wait until our next session. You are encouraged to stay in touch via e-mail as this provides an accessible way for me to monitor your progress, and to add extra insights during your coaching journey.

- **Communication**   I will always reply to your communications within 48 hours (except when out of town or on holidays, and I do my best to notify my clients of such dates). Even if no specific feedback is required or necessary, I will (at the very least) acknowledge the receipt of your communications.

From *The Coaching Starter Kit* by CoachVille.com, published by W. W. Norton & Company, Inc.
Form courtesy of and copyrighted by Pavla Michaela Polcarova, CPR Coaching Services

49

- **Commitment and Integrity**   If I make a promise to you, this promise will be kept—in the way promised and in the time frame promised. If, in exceptional circumstances only, I am unable to keep a commitment, I will notify you of this as soon as I know of the need for change. I will coach you at the highest standards of integrity, honesty, professionalism, and respect. As I am adamant about delivering high value to my clients, I will let you know if I feel that my involvement is not likely to make a positive difference in your life and/or business.

- **Nonjudgmental Attitude**   I am not here to judge right or wrong. My position is to coach you to get the life you want. As there may be times when you will share information that may make you vulnerable, I assure you that I will treat your choices and actions (past, present, or future) with respect.

- **Tenacity about Your Progress**   As you have hired me to help you grow, I believe that some of the most valuable coaching I can deliver to you comes through the tough places you may be unwilling to visit on your own: honest feedback, challenging questions, assignments designed to challenge your comfort zones, accountability to your commitments, and an occasional, usually gentle and always caring, "kick in the behind."

- **30-Day, Risk-Free Guarantee**   If within the first 30 days of our coaching relationship, you feel that the process is unlikely to make a difference in your life and/or business, please let me know and I will cheerfully refund your fees to you.

WHAT YOU CAN EXPECT OF YOURSELF AND THE COACHING EXPERIENCE

Just as if you were to read an exciting book, it is sometimes best not to know what exactly is ahead of you. It is up to you to let me know the results that you want from our coaching sessions. It is up to me to plan the steps to take you to those results, and it is up to us, together, to make sure the steps are taken and all necessary adjustments are made as we go along. Our sessions are used to debrief on past assignments, ask and answer questions, strategize, and set up steps.

In my experience, almost every client will pass through periods of feeling completely invincible (and will generally fly through all given assignments, and other periods of feeling fearful, doubtful, tired, or even resentful of the process. I personally get excited to see all of these times because they all form part of the necessary growth cycle. To you, some periods of coaching may feel great and others you would rather do without. Overall however, the growth curve will be positive. Many clients report some or all of the following: increased earnings, better use of time, better physical shape, better relationships, better health, more free time, and always an overall huge increase in their sense of control and peace of mind.

WHAT I WOULD LIKE TO ASK OF YOU

- **Timeliness**   It is important for us to keep our appointments for your benefit, as well as the benefit of my other clients. Twenty-four-hour notice is required to cancel an appointment; I reserve the right to charge for a session cancelled with less notice than this. If you are delayed for an appointment, please call me to let me know. I do my best to schedule clients with enough buffer time on either side of an appointment, but in some situations a delayed appointment will mean that our session will have to be cut short.

From *The Coaching Starter Kit* by CoachVille.com, published by W. W. Norton & Company, Inc.
Form courtesy of and copyrighted by Pavla Michaela Polcarova, CPR Coaching Services

- **Completion of Assignments** It is up to you to complete assignments as given. Whenever possible, I would appreciate getting your assignment at least a day before our session so that I can go over it before we meet again. The bottom line is that clients who diligently complete their assignments outside of our sessions get far more out of the coaching program. It is much easier to build a house on top of a solid foundation, so each assignment affects the next one. I also have more fun watching my clients get great results than average ones!

- **Feedback** Give and ask for feedback as much as possible. Let me know when something is working for you, as well as when something is not; the earlier the better. When you want specific or more in-depth feedback on something you are working on, please ask. Although telepathy is a somewhat necessary part of my work, direct feedback is the easiest way to ensure that you get what you need.

- **Fees** For prepaid programs, coaching fees are due before our first session. For monthly programs, coaching fees are due at the beginning of each month. When fees are agreed to and paid up front, we can then focus our sessions on the real task at hand—getting you the results you want.

- **Referrals** Many of my clients choose to refer my services to others. I like to ask for referrals outside of our coaching sessions so that the focus of our work is exclusively on you and the results you want. Whether you choose to refer people to me or not, I would like you to know how the referral process works. As you have experienced, I will first have a discussion with anyone who is interested in my services so that we can both determine if there is a good fit between their needs and my expertise. If there is a fit, they will become clients. If there isn't a good fit, I will do my best to offer your referral to a coach who will better fit their needs and goals. In all cases, I do my best to place your referral, so feel free to refer anyone who is looking to improve their life or business and I will make sure they get the right coach for their needs. Referrals form a substantial part of my practice and they come from clients whose trust I have worked hard to build, so you can be assured that I will go out of my way to take good care of anyone you choose to refer.

Again, congratulations on choosing to take part in the coaching program, and I sincerely look forward to working with you and watching you get the life you want.

Welcome Packet

Read the information and follow the instructions on each page.

Dear _____ ,

Welcome to coaching! I enjoyed our recent conversation, and want to commend you for making a commitment to move forward with coaching at this time in your life. I am delighted that you have chosen me as your coach—thanks!

This welcome packet includes the following forms on the next five pages:

- Personal Information

- Reflection Questions

- What Am I Tolerating? Where Am I Procrastinating?

- Basic Coaching Guidelines & Agreement

- Basic TeleCoaching Guidelines & Agreement

Previous clients have found that the reflection questions take some time, so you may want to spread out your reflection, doing a little each day over the period of several days. Bullets or phrases are a good way to respond. Take as much or as little space as you wish. By doing this work prior to our initial session, you will begin to focus on the current reality and on your future vision of yourself and your life.

I have a few requests to make:

1. Please fill out these forms and e-mail or fax them back to me so that I will have them the day before our initial session.

2. Please bring these forms along with your calendar, so that we can set appointments for the month.

3. Please bring the initial session fee of $ _____, payable to _____ .

4. Enjoy this time of preparation!

I'm looking forward to meeting with you on _____ from _____ . In the interim, should you have any questions or concerns, please let me know, because I'm here for you!

My best,

_____

From *The Coaching Starter Kit* by CoachVille.com, published by W. W. Norton & Company, Inc.

53

Personal Information

All personal information is confidential and treated appropriately.

Name
_____

Home address
_____

Home
_____

Telephone
_____

E-mail address
_____

Fax (H or W); is either ok?
_____

Occupation
_____

Employer
_____

Work address
_____

Work telephone
_____

Cell/pager
_____

Date of birth
_____

Marital status
_____

Partner's name
_____

Names/Ages of children
_____

Reflection Questions

Please answer these questions as clearly and thoughtfully as possible, expressing the fullness of who you are. These are pondering questions designed to stimulate your self-discovery and to make work with your coach more productive. Submit your answers to your coach at least three days before your first session.

1. Why are you hiring a coach? Please place an asterisk next to the primary reason.

_____

_____

_____

2. What do you expect from me in my role as coach?

_____

_____

_____

3. What can I expect from you in this coaching relationship?

_____

_____

_____

4. What Is your life's purpose or mission? How do you stay faithful to that?

_____

_____

_____

5. What are you passionate about, gets your blood pumping, or gives you joy?

_____

_____

_____

6. If life were "as good as it gets"—what's there? If your job were "as good as it gets"—what's there?

_____

_____

_____

From *The Coaching Starter Kit* by CoachVille.com, published by W. W. Norton & Company, Inc.

57

7. In order for me to effectively coach you, what should I know about you? About how you think or operate? About how you reach decisions? About what motivates you?

_____

_____

_____

8. What is your Myers-Briggs personality type, if you know it? If you don't know it, or are not familiar with this test, would you like me to do this inventory with you at a later date?

_____

_____

_____

9. What's missing from your life that you could add to make it complete?

_____

_____

_____

10. What's present in your life for which you are grateful?

_____

_____

_____

11. What are your values? Place an asterisk next to the one(s) you want to live out more fully.

_____

_____

_____

12. What adjectives describe who you are now, at your core? What adjectives describe who you want to be in the future?

_____

_____

_____

13. Lastly, what questions/concerns do you have about the coaching process?

_____

_____

_____

What Am I Tolerating? Where Am I Procrastinating?

People, things, and experiences sometimes cause our energy to leak out rather than to be tapped to meet our goals. What are you putting up with that drains your energy, whether you're consciously aware of it or not? Or, to phrase this question another way, on what are you procrastinating that if you accomplished you would feel very relieved?

Examples might be in the contexts of physical environment (home, office, car, wardrobe), health (food, exercise, doctor appointments), relationships, work, community service, money, etc.

Please list what you are tolerating or procrastinating in the space below. Brainstorm as many ideas as you can, and then identify the top ten that you might like to act upon for your own satisfaction and joy.

_____

_____

_____

_____

_____

_____

_____

1. _____

2. _____

3. _____

4. _____

5. _____

6. _____

7. _____

8. _____

9. _____

10. _____

From *The Coaching Starter Kit* by CoachVille.com, published by W. W. Norton & Company, Inc.

59

Basic Coaching Guidelines & Agreement

Welcome!	I have positive expectations for a coaching relationship that helps you to create the life you want to live. To partner together professionally, I want you to be familiar with the following guidelines.
Terms of Coaching	I invite you to think of coaching as a process. Many people create change for themselves in a short time; however, to refine and sustain the change takes several months. So, I begin the coaching process with a 3-month commitment on the part of both of us.
Fees	My coaching fee is $ _____ per month, payable to _____, and received in my office by the first day of the month. My fee for the initial session is $ _____, due on the day of the initial session. Your coaching fee includes: 3 scheduled sessions or calls per month, each for 45 minutes at a scheduled time; e-mails if desired between sessions; and 5-10 minute calls as needed. The sessions will be held weekly, typically the first 3 weeks of the month.
Procedure	You will call me at the agreed upon time. If I am out of town at the time of our appointment, I will give you a number to reach me. If you wish to connect with me in between sessions with a challenge, a success, or an inquiry, I will make every attempt to respond to your call or e-mail within 24 hours on weekdays. Please limit these calls to 5-10 minutes. I'm happy to provide this extra level of service at no additional charge.
Changes	If you need to reschedule our appointment, please give me 24 hours notice. Unless there is an emergency, if you do not show up for a scheduled call, we will not make up that time. If I need to reschedule our appointment, I will give you at least 24 hours notice as well.
Problems	If I ever say or do anything that upsets you or doesn't feel right, please bring it to my attention so that we can resolve it as soon as possible. My objective is to have a coaching relationship that is fully open, honest, real, and trusting in our communication styles.

From *The Coaching Starter Kit* by CoachVille.com, published by W.W. Norton & Company, Inc.

61

Basic TeleCoaching Guidelines & Agreement

Fill in the spaces with the appropriate information. Put a check mark in the boxes where applicable. Applicant's signature and payment information must be completed at bottom of application, prior to approval.

Session Day/Time	Day and time of sessions will be agreed upon and scheduled, to be repeated monthly. Any changes must be made via telephone and confirmed either by fax or e-mail at least 24 hours in advance.
Session Options	❑ 45 minutes $ _____ /mo ❑ 60 minutes $ _____ /mo Note: One time "intake" charge of $ _____ will be assessed at the onset of the coaching program—includes one-on-one debriefing and initial goal setting session. Charges are based on 3 sessions per month/36 sessions per year. ❑ On-site or travel required. Additional charge of $ _____ /month will apply.
Call Procedure	The coach will call the client at the prearranged number on the day and time scheduled. The coach will be responsible for all telephone-related charges. The allotted time will begin when the call is placed. Should the coach be placed on hold, this time will be counted as part of the allotted time.
Termination	This agreement is for 6 months and may be extended on a month-to-month basis following the initial 6 months with the mutual agreement of both parties. Should the client or the coach determine that insufficient progress or cooperation exists after the initial 90-day period, either party may cancel this agreement without recourse, other than full payment for the period to date. Cancellations must be in writing and may be delivered by fax or e-mail. In the event of fees owed at the time of cancellation, full payment is due.
Confidentiality	The coach recognizes that certain information of a confidential manner may be relayed during either regular or coach-on-call sessions. The coach will not at any time, either directly or indirectly, use this information for the coach's benefit or disclose said information to anyone else without specific client approval (excludes disclosure of illegal or unethical activities).
Nature of Relationship	The coach has a background and expertise in _____. The client has been made aware that the COACHING RELATIONSHIP IS IN NO WAY TO BE CONSIDERED OR CONSTRUED AS PSYCHOLOGICAL COUNSELING OR ANY TYPE OF THERAPY. The client has also been made aware that coaching results cannot be guaranteed. The client agrees that he/she is entering into coaching with the understanding that they are responsible for their own results. The client also agrees to hold the coach free of all liability and responsibility for any adverse situations created as a direct or indirect result of specific referral or advice given by the coach.

From *The Coaching Starter Kit* by CoachVille.com, published by W. W. Norton & Company, Inc.
Form courtesy of and copyrighted by Business Development Specialists, Inc.

APPLICANT'S INFORMATION:

Name _____

Position/Title _____ Company _____

Street Address _____ City _____

State _____ Zip Code _____

Telephone _____ Fax _____

E-mail Address _____

Credit Card # _____ Exp. Date _____ ❑ Am Exp. ❑ MC/VISA

Signature of Client _____ Signature of Credit Card Holder _____

Application Date _____ Approval Date _____

Signature of Coach _____

Coaching Fast Start

Here are some intriguing questions to ponder in preparation for our first session together. I would also like you to choose three goals that we can work on together over the next ninety days. Remember, this is only the beginning of the path to discovery that will enable you to make the most of who you are. Please type up your responses and fax or e-mail them to me before we start.

1. What have you been procrastinating about lately? Can you list ten things?

_____

_____

_____

_____

2. What is the most important thing you learned this past year?

_____

_____

_____

_____

3. What do you consider to be your best strengths? (Or, if you like, what are the gifts you have around which you have oriented your life?)

_____

_____

_____

_____

4. If you were not doing what you do now, what would you like to be doing?

_____

_____

_____

_____

From *The Coaching Starter Kit* by Coachville.com, published by W. W. Norton & Company, inc.
Form courtesy of and copyrighted by Brian Philcox

5. What characteristic or trait do you find most appealing in others?

_____

_____

_____

_____

_____

6. What is it you think you had as a child that you do not have now?

_____

_____

_____

_____

_____

7. If you were guaranteed success, what would you do?

_____

_____

_____

_____

_____

8. What talents do you have that few, if any, see?

_____

_____

_____

_____

_____

STARTING BUDGET
90-Day Budget

Be conservative, not optimistic. A coaching practice always takes longer to establish than you think. Keep your day job. Create your 90-day plan by filling in the spaces below.

	MONTH 1	MONTH 2	MONTH 3	
Income				
Coaching clients	_____	_____	_____	+_____
Workshop/Seminars	_____	_____	_____	+_____
Speaking engagements	_____	_____	_____	+_____
Other _____	_____	_____	_____	+_____
Other _____	_____	_____	_____	+_____
❑ Total Income	_____	_____	_____	= A_____
Expenses				
Telephone, voice-mail	_____	_____	_____	+_____
Printing, materials, brochure	_____	_____	_____	+_____
Promotional	_____	_____	_____	+_____
Coaching fee expenses	_____	_____	_____	+_____
Training seminar/books	_____	_____	_____	+_____
Office rent/payments	_____	_____	_____	+_____
Other _____	_____	_____	_____	+_____
❑ Other _____	_____	_____	_____	+_____
❑ Total Expenses	_____	_____	_____	= B_____
Total Startup Expenses	_____	_____	_____	= C_____
Net Profit from Coaching	_____	_____	_____	= (A-B-C)_____

From *The Coaching Starter Kit* by CoachVille.com, published by W. W. Norton & Company, Inc.

67

Start-Up Budget for a Coaching Practice

Allow between $2,500 to $5,000 to do it right. Create your budget by filling in the spaces below.

MATERIALS	BUDGET	PRICE RANGE
❑ 1,000 business cards	$	$ 10–500
❑ 500 letterhead and envelopes	$	$ 100–500
❑ Office supplies	$	$ 100–500
❑ Brochures	$	$ 100–500

EQUIPMENT	BUDGET	
❑ High quality telephone	$	$ 50–200
❑ Separate phone line	$	$ 50–200
❑ Fax machine	$	$ 300–2000
❑ Computer	$	$ 500–4000
❑ Software	$	$ 500–1000
❑ Printer	$	$ 300–2000
❑ Large table or desk	$	$ 50–1000
❑ Ergonomic chair	$	$ 100–500
❑ Telephone headset (a must)	$	$ 75–250
❑ Large file cabinet	$	$ 50–350
❑ High quality lamp	$	$ 50–200
❑ High quality answering machine	$	$ 50–200

TOTAL $

From *The Coaching Starter Kit* by CoachVille.com, published by W. W. Norton & Company, Inc.
Form courtesy of and copyrighted by Michelle Schubnel

Chapter 3

The First Session

WHERE TO START

First Session Agenda

Client _____ Session Number _____

Date _____ Time _____

Format (in person/phone)_____

BEFORE THE SESSION

❏ Review the previous session or activity with this client.

❏ Review any previously taken notes on prospect. _____

_____

STARTING THE SESSION

❏ Hi, how are you? Thanks for your interest in life coaching.

❏ So, tell me a little about yourself.

_____

_____

_____

_____

_____

❏ What's your greatest challenge right now? _____

❏ What motivates you in your life right now?_____

❏ What are you tolerating? _____

❏ What are you willing to do in the next 30 days? _____

TOWARDS THE END OF THE SESSION

❏ Give one great insight, tip, tool, or action—use your intuition _____

❏ Ask prospect if they would like to proceed with life coaching for next ____ months: ❏ YES ❏ NO

❏ If not, why not? _____

❏ We have about 5 minutes left, let's review what actions you are going to take:

_____ _____

_____ _____

❏ What's one thing you have gotten out of today's session? _____

❏ Confirm next session date, time, and format_____

AFTER THE CALL

❏ Send fieldwork (homework) via e-mail and file this form

From *The Coaching Starter Kit* by CoachVille.com, published by W. W. Norton & Company, Inc.
Form courtesy of and copyrighted by Belinda Merry

Coaching Prep Tips

Read and understand the following.

INTRODUCTION

You may come to your first coaching call without preparing, if you wish. Coaching can be equally effective with or without preparation, but many clients enjoy getting ready. The steps and suggestions below should help.

1. **Write down a list of at least twenty things you are tolerating.**

   Most clients want to get busy on their goals right away, but I often recommend they first start (or concurrently work on) what they are putting up with. It is hard to move forward when you are drained by present tolerations.

2. **Make a list of the five outcomes you want to enjoy within the next ninety days.**

   What do you most want to have happen in your personal and/or professional life within ninety days? What is going to make the biggest difference to you? What will have made your coaching worthwhile? Please be as specific and as measurable as possible, and please select outcomes which are doable and which do not depend on others to occur.

3. **Identify one or more of the 100-point checklists to focus on.**

   Most clients like working on one or more of the client forms, such as Resources and Assets, Revising Your Communication Style, and Special Project. Some of these programs will strengthen you and your life (Resources and Assets); others will guide and direct you (Special Project); others will train you (Revising Your Communication Style). Pick one or several of these client forms—they will provide a focus and support structure between your coaching sessions.

4. **Write down three fundamental changes you need to make in order to become more successful.**

   You probably already know these, and it is good to articulate them.

5. **Ask your friends and family what they feel you could/should work on with your coach.**

   You should do this for two reasons. First, your family and friends know you and have a perspective that is hard to have about yourself, so it's very valuable to know what they are thinking about your work and life. Second, it is extremely helpful to tell people you have a coach and are coaching. Some clients want to keep this a secret (and I can understand why), but I have found that clients progress faster when they share with others what they are changing, improving, and working on. Sharing creates synergy and support. Secrets restrict the energy.

From *The Coaching Starter Kit* by CoachVille.com, published by W. W. Norton & Company, Inc.

75

Top Issues with Which to Start

What should you and your client focus on first when starting your coaching? Here's a list of 9 areas where the coach and client can start.

1. Tolerations

Ask the client to make a list of what he/she is putting up with. There will be many things on this list on which to help the client focus. When the client starts getting rid of tolerations, he/she will feel like he/she is making progress in his/her life, and the momentum created (because energy is freed up) will keep the client motivated, which is very important when a client is new to coaching.

2. Shoulds

Find out what the client thinks he/she should be doing right now, personally and professionally. Ask the client to make a list of at least 10 shoulds. This educates the client to quickly find out how much of life he/she is living and how much of someone else's life he/she is living.

3. Frustrations

What is frustrating the client? Ask the client "What are the 5 things that are frustrating you right now about yourself, your life, your work, or others?" Feelings are a great place to start the coaching process because when the client gets in touch with and shares real feelings, the truth begins to come out. And when the truth comes out, there is relief and movement. Let truth drive your client, not you.

4. Money

Money—or the lack of it—is at the heart of at least 50% of a client's current problems, whether they recognize it or not. Find out how much the client makes, how much they owe, how much they are saving, and if the client is willing to make some financial changes, quickly. If he/she is, stress is usually reduced right away, and this frees him/her up to better benefit from your coaching.

5. Desires

What does your client really want in his/her personal or business life? What goal has he/she given up on or put off for a while due to circumstances? When a client feels that someone (the coach) cares enough to encourage him/her to reach for what will bring the greatest happiness, it may be all the client needs to succeed in that area. Remember, success is stressful, and getting what you want is sometimes a stretch; that's why the client has hired you—to help him/her get through whatever is in the way. When you help the client tap into what they want most, they are inspired and do not need constant motivation.

From *The Coaching Starter Kit* by CoachVille.com, published by W. W. Norton & Company, Inc.

77

6. Integrity

It is very important to determine the strength of your client's integrity. In other words, is your client doing the best for themselves and their body? Are they stressed out, eating/drinking too much, running on adrenaline, stepping over problems, avoiding the truth in a situation, or not taking time for himself/herself? Without enough integrity, whatever you help the client to achieve will eventually fade because the "container" for their life is cracked.

7. Outcomes

Many clients know exactly what they want and they want your support to achieve it, so by all means, help them reach these outcomes. You can definitely focus with a client on outcomes, but also weave in some of the other 8 starting points into your coaching (always get the client's permission). Some clients are very happy with a single focus of achieving outcomes, and they really do not want to work on the intangible.

8. Strategies

Some clients want you to help them develop a strategy or a plan so they can achieve their result in the shortest period of time, with the least stress. If the client asks you how they can achieve X, then you know they are asking for a strategy. Sometimes the client will ask what action steps they should take, but you may want to work with them on strategy development first because with the right strategy, the steps become obvious.

9. A Change or Improvement

Most clients want to change or improve something. For example, they may want to change jobs or improve a relationship. The trick is to discover if their "change goal" is what they really want, or if it is something they want to do because it will get them something else, as in "If I get a promotion, I'll be more fulfilled." As a coach, you might want to work with the client on values first to find out what would fulfill them, because a promotion may not be the ticket.

From *The Coaching Starter Kit* by CoachVille.com, published by W. W. Norton & Company, Inc.

Coach's Mission Statement

MY EXPECTATION IS

- That you shall have more of what you truly want in your life.

MY COMMITMENT IS

- I will listen very carefully to what you do say and what you do not say.

- I will ask questions until I am certain that you and I understand you.

- I will be absolutely truthful at all times.

- I believe that you can accomplish more than you believe that you can.

- I will have high expectations, and will ask you to reach for them.

- I will support you and your decisions, absolutely.

- I will challenge you to reach for an even more fulfilling life.

- I may sometimes offer suggestions, but I am not a therapist, financial advisor, or business consultant; therefore, all decisions are yours.

- Everything we say remains confidential.

- You will receive more than what is promised.

WE WILL BE SUCCESSFUL

- Because the synergy of having two brains working for you always increases your effectiveness.

MY FEES ARE

- $ _____ per hour for corporate clients and $ _____ for individuals. This covers the hour or so each time we meet and includes an occasional phone call, travel time, parking, miscellaneous expenses, and whatever additional time or research that I may opt to do on my own.

YOU

- Are encouraged to make a 3-month commitment to yourself, but you are free to end the relationship at any time. Should you elect to end the relationship during a session, there will be no charge for that session.

From *The Coaching Starter Kit* by CoachVille.com, published by W. W. Norton & Company, Inc.
Form courtesy of and copyrighted by Dave Lambert, Personal Business Coach

The following are answers to frequently asked questions about how our coaching relationship is going to work and how to get the most out of coaching.

Dear Client:

COMPUTER LITERACY

You will need some basic e-mail skills if you wish to keep in touch via e-mail between coaching sessions. At the minimum, you need to be able to:

- Receive and read e-mail

- Reply to e-mail

- Reply to e-mail by typing within the original e-mail message

If you do not have the above skills, please let me know and I will walk you through them during our session.

COACHING FAST START

Please fill out this form, prior to our second telephone call; this is imperative to making coaching effective. The form will save time, and give focus to the coaching sessions.

NUMBER OF COACHING SESSIONS PER MONTH

You receive four coaching sessions per month. Sometimes there may be a fifth Monday, Tuesday, etc. in the month, but we will not coach on those days (this happens four times a year).

LENGTH OF COACHING SESSIONS

Coaching sessions run 25-30 minutes. I usually have another client calling in at the end of our session, so we will need to end on time. I will let you know about ten minutes before the end of our time, so you will not feel rushed.

GETTING THE MOST OUT OF COACHING BY SUMMARIZING

You will get out of coaching what you can retain and put to use in your life. To that end, in the last five minutes of the call, I will ask you to summarize what you learned, what was valuable, and what you are going to do as a result of the day's coaching session.

POST CALL NOTES

Some clients take notes of our sessions because they want to refer to them during the week, and some clients e-mail or fax those notes to me so I can read them by the next session. This is entirely up to you.

From *The Coaching Starter Kit* by CoachVille.com, published by W. W. Norton & Company, Inc.
Form courtesy of and copyrighted by Rinatta Paries, Relationship Coach

ADDITIONAL CONTACT

E-mail contact is included in our coaching relationship. You may e-mail me at any time and as much as you would like to ask questions, share wins, ask for support, or for any other reason. Brief, unscheduled phone contact is also included in our coaching relationship. Please feel free to call me when you need me or want to check in, as long as you keep unscheduled calls to 10 minutes.

HANDLING PAYMENT

Payment for coaching is due on the agreed upon date. If paying by check, please mail your check seven days ahead, to make sure I receive it on time. When I receive and process your check you will get an e-mail confirmation. If I do not receive your check on time, you will be notified by e-mail and asked to remedy the situation. If money or bill paying is currently a problem, let's focus on that during our coaching.

ENDING COACHING

Naturally, all clients complete their coaching with me at some point. Clients work with me for about three months to five years, with the average client staying about eighteen months. I expect you to leave when you no longer get the value you wish, or when you need a break. This is a part of my business and is perfectly normal. If you feel it is time to leave, please communicate freely with me. I do ask that you give me a two-week notice, so that we may have time to complete.

WHAT ARE YOU PAYING FOR?

In coaching, you are paying for information, advice, support, collaboration, strategies, continuous presence, energy, creativity, availability, and partnership—not necessarily just time or the number of coaching sessions. You can get as much value from 10 minutes of coaching as you can from three hours of coaching; it all depends on timing, openness, and synergy.

I hope that this outline of services and procedures has been helpful. If there is something important to you that I have not covered above, please let me know and I will be happy to clarify it for you.

Warmly,

From *The Coaching Starter Kit* by CoachVille.com, published by W. W. Norton & Company, Inc.
Form courtesy of and copyrighted by Rinatta Paries, Relationship Coach

Client Welcome (for TeleCoaching)

You have chosen to use me as your coach. I appreciate the opportunity to work with you. I have prepared the following coaching Q & A and the enclosed materials to assist you in getting the most from your time and out of our relationship.

WHAT IS COACHING?

Coaching is a form of consulting. Like a consultant, a coach helps you and/or your firm to:

- Solve problems
- Reach goals
- Design a plan of action
- Make decisions

In addition to the above, the coach "stays with" (coaches) the client to:

- Implement the plan of action, working through the inevitable changes and any obstacles.
- Maintain a healthy balance between the client's personal and professional life.
- Keep looking ahead to take advantage of opportunities which are just now formulating.
- Bring out the client's personal best, keeping focused on his/her needs, values, and vision.

All coaches are consultants; few consultants are coaches.

WHAT TYPE OF GOALS CAN A COACH HELP ME TO ACHIEVE?

Every coach has several specialties. That is, they are trained and experienced in helping clients reach several types of goals. All told, there are over 40 coaching specialties. I work with:

Entrepreneurs who are at one of the following places with their business:

- Want to double sales or profits? Ready to blow the roof off? Fully committed but need a specific plan of action? Want strategic planning to make the most of the resources you have?

- In trouble? Can't meet the payroll? Are sales declining? Problems with key staff? Having personal conflicts or problems? Too much stress? Business too successful, too fast? Time and prioritizing problems? Ready to bankrupt?

- Making changes? Adding a new product or service? Starting a new business? Wanting to shift your focus from one area to another?

I also train those wanting to be coaches and to develop a full practice.

Professionals like stockbrokers, realtors, trainers, therapists, sales representatives, consultants, and health professionals such as physicians, chiropractors, and others who:

- Want a full practice. Ready to be full? Upgrade your clientele? Become irresistibly attractive rather than promotion-based? Find and develop a high-level referral network?

- Are ready to be leaders. I work with pros who want to be #1 in their firm, recognized as masters in their field, and/or develop a model reputation.

- Are committed to being financially independent, sooner. Professionals and entrepreneurs are uniquely positioned to make a lot of money. My job is to help you make more and keep much more.

Managers and Executives responsible for the success of a sales team, branch, or division who need to:

- Reach high targets and quotas. Accomplishing this consistently requires a manager who also coaches the team to work together to reach goals. I coach managers and executives and show them how to coach their people to reach these targets.

- Pull off large projects. Successfully completing projects and implementing programs such as enhanced customer-service takes focus—having your own coach can make the process easier. It helps to have someone to speak with as you face this type of challenge.

- Increase productivity, substantially. No longer an option, substantially increasing productivity is a primary focus for many firms. A coach advises on how to upgrade the company culture, develop teamwork based on values, align departmental goals with the company's mission, and shift the firm to be innovative and profit driven.

WHY DOES COACHING WORK?

Coaching works because it brings out your best. A coach believes you have the answers and is trained to bring them out (painlessly)!

Specifically, this is what I do during our coaching sessions:

Listen.   I listen fully. You are the focus. I listen to what you say, what you are trying to say, and what you are not saying.

Share.   After you have fully communicated, I share with you my advice, ideas, comments, and views on your situation, dilemma, or opportunity.

Endorse.   Anyone who's up to something—an entrepreneur, a manager with an extraordinary objective, or a professional filling the practice—needs an outside voice full of endorsement, compassion, and acknowledgment. Not as a yes-man, but as someone who knows what it takes to achieve.

Suggest.   I want a lot for you. I want you to be healthy, happy, and successful. I want you to be on a strong financial track. I want you to enjoy your family and friends. I want you to have a life that inspires others—and yourself. Part of my job is to be at least three steps ahead of you, yet be with you. As such, I make requests and suggestions.

WHAT IS THE FEE?

I charge $ _____ per hour.

HOW DO YOU WORK?

I work primarily on the telephone: it is called telecoaching. You call me at a local or toll-free number at a pre-scheduled time. Most clients call me once per week at the same time each week. Calls last twenty-five or fifty-five minutes. The monthly fee, payable in advance, for the twenty-five minute call is $ _____; for the fifty-five minute call, $ _____. Additional time is billed at $ _____ per hour. Clients may meet with me, but most find the telephone to be more efficient.

WHAT OTHER SERVICES DO YOU OFFER?

In addition to coaching and telecoaching, I:

- Lead workshops and trainings.
- Deliver presentations and keynotes (i.e. coaching employees for productivity, entrepreneurial success, goal setting, from transition to on-track, and others).
- Assist with business proposals (i.e. loan packages, business plans, corporate sales proposals, project outlines, and others).
- Write seminars and programs (public seminars, corporate training programs, and others).

WHAT CREDENTIALS DO YOU HAVE IN ORDER TO COACH?

The primary credentials of any coach is the assessable success of his or her clients. Additionally, I have:

(list your credentials here)

Currently, I work with _____ clients. References are available upon request.

WHAT ELSE SHOULD I KNOW ABOUT HOW YOU WORK?

There are several administrative guidelines that you should know:

1. Fees are paid in advance, due on the 1st of each month.

2. Your time slot is your time slot. Please don't try to reschedule. If you are going on vacation or can't make a call one week, we will make up the time before you leave or after you return. From time to time when you call, you may get my voice mail asking that you call another number. This number will be a local call or the toll-free number. The toll-free number "follows me" to wherever I am, since I lead workshops in New York, Houston, Florida, and California.

3. The monthly fee covers four sessions per month. And, every three months, there's an extra week on the calendar. I take that time off to restore and there is no coaching call.

WHAT DO YOU EXPECT OF YOUR CLIENTS?

I ask that you grant our relationship enough room so that you can reach your goals quickly. What that means is that you are willing to tell me all of what you are thinking and feeling, and that you are willing to listen to what I have to say. And, you should take the time you want to develop the trust you need between us.

WHAT CAN I EXPECT FROM YOU, AS THE COACH?

You can expect me to be:

- Unconditionally constructive. No matter what happens during our call, you can expect me to say only those things which further your life and your goals. If you are disturbed, I do understand. If you are stuck, I will be patient. If you can't wait to share a victory, I will celebrate with you. I will not make you wrong, criticize you, complain to you, or gossip about you.

- Straightforward. Yes, one can be unconditionally constructive and still speak straight. From time to time, I will ask you to begin, end, or modify something. And, I will honor your right to refuse.

ABOUT CONFIDENTIALITY?

A coach doesn't gossip. That means that what you are doing, how you are doing, what you have accomplished, and your personal secrets are not discussed or hinted at by me to anyone else. From time to time, the person who referred you to me may ask how you are doing. My stock answer: "He/she is doing just fine." (Period.)

My client list is confidential. People may know you are working with me, but that information won't come from me.

SPEAKING OF REFERRALS . . .

My practice fills by referrals. If you are benefiting from our relationship, I would appreciate you suggesting that appropriate colleagues and friends of yours speak with me.

I know many full-time coaches practicing in the U.S. I will be happy to speak with anyone you send me, and I will introduce them to the coach who I think is qualified to handle their needs, whether it is me or another coach.

Thanks!

Thanks for the chance to serve. Please fill out the Welcome Packet and return to me ASAP.

From *The Coaching Starter Kit* by CoachVille.com, published by W. W. Norton & Company, Inc.

85

Welcome

I am pleased to welcome you as a client. I look forward to helping you achieve greatness. Please complete the items checked and return to me the documents indicated.

❑   Send your check for $ _____ today, for the month of _____ , if you haven't done so already.

❑   Please complete the enclosed Client Questionnaire and Agreement on the following two pages, then make and send me a copy of them. Put your originals in a file folder marked Coaching.

❑   Read the enclosed Policies and Procedures so you'll know how best to use me.

OUR CALLS ARE SCHEDULED FOR:

Day_____

Date_____

From _____   to _____ P M C E time

Call me at ( ) _____ – _____

I look forward to speaking with you at that time.

Warmest regards,

_____

From *The Coaching Starter Kit* by CoachVille.com, published by W.W. Norton & Company, Inc.

87

Client Questionnaire

Read and fill in the necessary information.

As your coach, it is important for me to understand who you are, what you value, and how you approach life. As such, I developed this questionnaire with a variety of pondering-type inquiries designed to promote exploration about what you really want out of life. Please set aside some time to thoroughly consider these questions, and then fax or e-mail your responses to me prior to our initial session (I will also send you these questions via e-mail). Thanks!

Name: _____ Birthday: _____

Mailing Address: _____

City/State/Zip: _____

Telephone – Day: _____ Telephone – Eve: _____

Telephone – Mobile: _____ E-mail: _____

Best time/place to reach you: _____

1. Why have you hired me?

_____
_____
_____
_____

2. What are the primary short-term goals that you want to focus on in the next ninety days? (Please indicate the date by which you would like to achieve each goal.)

Goal 1: _____ Date: _____
Goal 2: _____ Date: _____
Goal 3: _____ Date: _____
Goal 4: _____ Date: _____
Goal 5: _____ Date: _____
Goal 6: _____ Date: _____
Goal 7: _____ Date: _____
Goal 8: _____ Date: _____
Goal 9: _____ Date: _____
Goal 10: _____ Date: _____

From *The Coaching Starter Kit* by CoachVille.com, published by W.W. Norton & Company, Inc.
Form courtesy of and copyrighted by Michelle Schubnel

89

3. What long-term goals do you want to focus on in our coaching? (Only choose things that you really want, not what you feel you should do!)

_____

_____

_____

_____

4. What would you like to do or accomplish during your lifetime (personally or professionally), in order to consider your life well lived, with few or no regrets?

_____

_____

_____

_____

5. What is your passion in life, or what makes you happiest and most fulfilled?

_____

_____

_____

_____

6. What are your favorite pastimes? (name at least five)

_____

_____

_____

_____

7. What motivates you or gives you energy? (i.e., deadlines, caffeine, your values, meditation, exercise, nature, status, adrenaline, etc.)

_____

_____

_____

_____

From *The Coaching Starter Kit* by CoachVille.com, published by W. W. Norton & Company, Inc.
Form courtesy of and copyrighted by Michelle Schubnel

8. What do you consider to be your personal and/or professional strengths?

_____

_____

_____

_____

9. Tell me five aspects of your personal/professional life, past or present, of which you are most proud.

_____

_____

_____

_____

10. Are you aware of any behaviors/beliefs that stand in the way of you achieving professional success and having a life you really love?

_____

_____

_____

_____

11. Tell me what I should know about you in order to coach you best.

_____

_____

_____

_____

12. How will you know that our coaching has been effective?

_____

_____

_____

_____

Agreement

Please review, adjust as necessary, sign where indicated, and return to the coach. Putting this in writing will strengthen your dedication.

Name _____

Initial term: _____ months, from _____ through _____

Fee $ _____ per hour $ _____ per month $ _____ for the project

Payment fees to be received in the office by the _____ of the month

BONUS AGREEMENT

Session day ❑ Mon ❑ Tue ❑ Wed ❑ Thu ❑ Fri ❑ Sat ❑ Sun

Session time _____ ❑ AM ❑ PM ❑ Pacific ❑ Mountain ❑ Central ❑ Eastern

Duration _____ minutes

CALL PROCEDURE

_____

_____

SERVICES PROVIDED

_____

_____

FOCUS OF WORK

_____

_____

GROUND RULES

1. Client calls the coach at scheduled time
2. Client pays coaching fees in advance
3. ❑ Client ❑ Coach pays for long distance charges, if any

OTHER TERMS ABOVE

_____

_____

Agreed to on _____

Client signature _____

Coach signature_____

From *The Coaching Starter Kit* by CoachVille.com, published by W. W. Norton & Company, Inc.

Policies & Procedures

COACHING FEE

$ _____ /month and $ _____ for the initial meeting. My preferred method of payment is by credit card authorization. I also accept payment by check, due on the first of the month. Make checks payable to _____ and mail to _____.

If paying by check, please mark your calendar to mail your payment on the 25th of each month, in lieu of a formal invoice.

HOW WE WILL MEET

We will meet by telephone (call me at _____) for thirty-five to forty-five minutes, three times each month. We will typically schedule our calls for the same time and day of the week for three weeks in a row. Weeks that we do not have scheduled calls are an excellent time for you to put extra time and effort into achieving your objectives.

CHANGES/CANCELLATIONS

I request that you make our scheduled coaching calls a priority. On the rare occasion when you need to reschedule, please let me know at least forty-eight hours in advance. Except in the case of an emergency, you will be charged for last-minute cancellations or missed calls.

EXTRA TIME

Please call or e-mail me between calls if you cannot wait to share a success, need advice, have a challenge, or just want to check in. I have time between our regular calls, and enjoy providing this extra level of service. I do not bill for this type of additional time, I only request that you keep extra calls to a maximum of five to ten minutes each.

INITIAL COACHING PERIOD

Although I do not make formal agreements with my clients, I recommend you commit to coaching for a minimum of three to six months. The benefits of coaching build over time. In order to make this experience as valuable as possible, I encourage you to make this commitment to yourself.

CONFIDENTIALITY

It is important for the integrity and value of our coaching relationship that we are open and honest with each other. In this light, what we discuss will remain completely confidential.

REFERRALS

Many of my clients have come to me by referral. If our coaching has enabled you to generate the results you want in your life, I ask that you please share your coaching experience with others, and refer me to anyone you know who might be interested in what coaching has to offer. I will happily conduct a complimentary thirty-minute coaching consultation with anyone you refer.

From *The Coaching Starter Kit* by CoachVille.com, published by W. W. Norton & Company, Inc.

95

Client Data

Complete the following data sheet.

Date Prepared _____

Name _____

Company _____

Address_____

City/State_____ Postal Code_____

Day Phone _____ Eve Phone _____

Voice-mail _____ Fax _____

Date of Birth _____

Occupation _____ Nature of Business/Position _____

Referred By _____

Initial Term month(s) _____

Start Date _____ Renewal Date _____

Rate $_____

Additional Time $_____

Bonus Agreement_____

Payment Due: On _____of month

Call Day & Time: M   T   W   Th   F   Sa   Su   _____ P M C E time for _____ minutes

Call Instructions _____

_____

Ground Rules

  1. Client calls and pays in advance.

  2. Coach has permission to be direct, though unconditionally constructive.

Other Terms_____

Above Agreed to on _____

Client Signature _____

Coach Signature _____

CLIENT QUESTIONNAIRES

Client Laser Questions: Creating Value in Coaching

Help the client to create value for himself/herself.

1. How will you know that you're getting more than your money's worth in our coaching?

_____

_____

_____

2. What changes will you need to make in order to make the most of what we talk about?

_____

_____

_____

3. How much stress is the monthly coaching fee going to cause you?

_____

_____

_____

4. What can I do for you during our sessions that is most empowering and helpful for you?

_____

_____

_____

5. Other than support and advice, what are five other ways I will be helping you most?

_____

_____

_____

6. What should I do/not do if you fall behind on your goals?

_____

_____

_____

From *The Coaching Starter Kit* by CoachVille.com, published by W. W. Norton & Company, Inc.

7. Would you like to be part of my TeleClasses, call me between sessions, or work on personal development programs as a part of our coaching?

_____

_____

_____

_____

8. What should we do or talk about toward the end of each coaching session?

_____

_____

_____

_____

9. What should I do if you miss a coaching session?

_____

_____

_____

_____

10. What would happen if we HADN'T started coaching?

_____

_____

_____

_____

11. What is the one regret that you don't want to have in this lifetime?

_____

_____

_____

_____

First Client Meeting Questionnaire

Read and answer the following questions.

What do you see yourself accomplishing as a result of our meeting today?

_____

_____

_____

_____

What are you going to do with the rest of your life?

_____

_____

_____

_____

Success means different things to different people. What's important about success to you?

_____

_____

_____

_____

If you could have anything you wanted—anything at all—what would it be?

_____

_____

_____

_____

What's important about money to you?

_____

_____

_____

_____

From *The Coaching Starter Kit* by CoachVille.com, published by W. W. Norton & Company, Inc.
Form courtesy of and copyrighted by Robert M. Miller, Dell Computer Corporation

If you were hurt or sick and couldn't work, how would you pay your bills?

_____

_____

_____

_____

Have you set goals and designed your retirement to last for as long as you live?

_____

_____

_____

_____

By what date do you want to be financially independent?

_____

_____

_____

_____

If we were having this discussion three years down the road, and you were looking back over that period, what has to happen for you to feel happy with your progress?

_____

_____

_____

_____

New Client Questionnaire

Please answer the following questions. Your answers will shape our coaching relationship, help you to get the most value from coaching, and help me get to know you.

1. How will you make sure that you get the most out of our coaching relationship?

_____

_____

2. Why did you hire me? In other words, what about me, what I offer, my experience, or my style, really works for you? What did you hear that made you go for coaching, and coaching with me?

_____

_____

3. What five things (people, results, states, resolutions, etc.) do you want most—right now in your life?

_____

_____

4. Which one of the above would you like us to start coaching on first?

_____

_____

5. What five things in your life are causing you discomfort/stress?

_____

_____

6. Which one is causing you the most discomfort/stress?

_____

_____

7. What else do you want me to know about you, your style, your needs, and what you need from me, as your coach?

_____

_____

_____

From *The Coaching Starter Kit* by CoachVille.com, published by W. W. Norton & Company, Inc.
Form courtesy of and copyrighted by Rinatta Paries, Relationship Coach

103

First Coaching Session

These are essential questions to ask.

1. What are you expecting from coaching?

   _____

   _____

2. What do you need most from me today?

   _____

   _____

3. What do you need most from me during our coaching?

   _____

   _____

4. What is the biggest change you are willing to make today?

   _____

   _____

5. What are the first three things you are going to do immediately after our session today?

   _____

   _____

6. How long will you be coaching with me?

   _____

   _____

7. How much of the work are you going to be willing to do during our sessions?

   _____

   _____

8. What is the one thing I should not say/do with you today?

   _____

   _____

9. What is the most exciting part of working with a coach?

   _____

   _____

10. What is the scariest part of working with a coach?

    _____

    _____

From *The Coaching Starter Kit* by CoachVille.com, published by W. W. Norton & Company, Inc.

105

About the Client

Find out what you can about the client, not just their goals or situation.

1. What are your three biggest concerns/fears about yourself?

_____

_____

2. What are your three biggest concerns/fears about life?

_____

_____

3. What are your three biggest concerns/fears about success?

_____

_____

4. What motivates you to want to improve/evolve?

_____

_____

5. What are the three most important things that you have learned about yourself?

_____

_____

6. What are you currently learning/accepting about yourself?

_____

_____

7. What is the best way to coach you?

_____

_____

8. In what areas are you foolish or irresponsible?

_____

_____

9. What is the best part of you? Why?

_____

_____

10. What habits do you have that make you feel badly about yourself?

_____

_____

Client's Life

Help the client to see their life more clearly.

1. Who or what is holding you back the most right now, and how?

_____

_____

_____

_____

2. How much stress are you under right now, and what is causing the stress?

_____

_____

_____

_____

3. What are the ten things that you are tolerating the most?

_____

_____

_____

_____

4. What about you makes your life work as well as it does?

_____

_____

_____

_____

5. Who are the key people in your life and what do they provide for you?

_____

_____

_____

_____

6. Is your life one of your own choosing?

_____

_____

_____

_____

From *The Coaching Starter Kit* by CoachVille.com, published by W.W. Norton & Company, Inc.

109

7. If not, which parts are not?

_____

_____

_____

_____

8. Is your life on an upward or downward trend?

_____

_____

_____

_____

9. What about your day do you like most?

_____

_____

_____

_____

10. What about your day do you like least?

_____

_____

_____

_____

11. What else, if anything, do you feel is important to accomplish in order for your life to be fulfilled and complete?

_____

_____

_____

_____

Client History

Every client has a history—you need to know it.

1. What have been your three most fulfilling accomplishments in life, thus far?

   _____

   _____

2. What was the biggest thing you have had to overcome?

   _____

   _____

3. How strong/powerful/healthy have your past personal or business role models been?

   _____

   _____

4. How have you failed, and how did that affect the way you think and act today?

   _____

   _____

5. Have you worked with a coach before? What worked? What did not work?

   _____

   _____

6. How have your attitudes about people and life changed over the past ten years?

   _____

   _____

7. What has made you the most successful or powerful?

   _____

   _____

8. Are you mostly past-, present-, or future-oriented?

   _____

   _____

9. What should I know about your professional background/history?

   _____

   _____

10. What should I know about your personal background/family history?

   _____

   _____

From *The Coaching Starter Kit* by CoachVille.com, published by W. W. Norton & Company, Inc.

Coaching Client Profile

Complete the following profile.

Client: _____ Intake Date: _____

❑ Male ❑ Female Age:_____ ❑ Married ❑ Domestic Partner ❑ Single ❑ Divorced ❑ Widow/er

Number of children: _____ Ages of children: _____

Education: ❑ HS ❑ Some college ❑ BA/BS ❑ MA/MS ❑ Ph.D.

Field of study: _____

Referred by: _____

Additional background: _____

_____

_____

Presenting issue: (What's been done? Impact? Relationships? Watch for own bias. Paraphrase.) _____

_____

_____

_____

_____

_____

_____

_____

_____

Distinction: _____

_____

_____

_____

_____

_____

_____

_____

_____

Goals/objectives:

❑ _____

❑ _____

❑ _____

❑ _____

❑ _____

From *The Coaching Starter Kit* by CoachVille.com, published by W. W. Norton & Company, Inc.
Form courtesy of and copyrighted by Kate Arendt, Genesis Consulting and Coaching

Part 2
Coaching Maintenance

Chapter 4

Coaching Recommendations

CONNECTING WITH THE CLIENT
7 Important Things to Know About Your Client

ASPECT #1

What they are not clear of.

A mentor of mine said once, "Our lives are spent doing what we are not clear of." Or, to restate: Until we get clear, we do the same things over and over again in a futile attempt to get clear so that we can move on and express our values.

ASPECT #2

What their four personal needs are.

Each of us has a unique set of critical needs that, until completely satisfied, keep us from reaching our potential.

Needs are those conditions in life that we must have to fully be ourselves. Assist the client to identify, articulate, and satisfy these critical needs. Most people are motivated—even compelled—by unsatisfied needs. Until these are fulfilled, coaching will be tough going for both parties.

ASPECT #3

What their special gifts are.

I believe that everyone has a special, unique gift to share with others. However, few people move far enough along the path of personal and professional development to be able to orient their lives around their gift.

Much of the work the coach does is to uncover the obstacles in the way of the client seeing that gift clearly.

ASPECT #4

What their core values are.

Values are those activities which turn you on, like creativity, learning, playing, loving, etc. Values are what we tend to do after our needs are met and after we are complete with the past. Values are not morals; values are our essence.

ASPECT #5

What they really want for themselves.

Most people do not know what they really want. Yes, they have a wish list and a "should want" list, but because most people still don't have their needs met and values clear, their wants are muddled or exaggerated. The coach can help a person discern what they really want—what will make them happy. These wants may be the same as their wish list (or very different); it's just that the person will want, not crave or need them. Wants are optional; they add to a life, they don't "give" life, as a value or need does.

ASPECT #6

How well they are doing in life's six areas.

Coaches can measure the quality of a person's life in six areas: relationships, health, career, money, recreation, and personal development. It is important to know exactly how a client is doing in all six areas so that you can direct the coaching to bring all areas up to the desired level (the tendency is to have one or two areas with low, low scores). But the coach needs to have an overview in order to make the biggest difference.

In the area of personal development, the coach should know the following six things about the client:

- How willing are they to grow and be more?
- How able are they to get what they want?
- How well does the client relate to others?
- How being-oriented is the person?
- How attracted is the person to what is possible?

ASPECT #7

What they want for others.

When we are well taken care of and in good shape, it is natural to want to give and assist others. Some people have a vision for others, or for the world that motivates them; others want the people around them to be happy and healthy. Anyway you look at it, it is a sign of advanced personal development when your client wants to help others, can afford it (time, love, money), and is motivated by choice (versus need or compulsiveness).

That's it! When you know and help the client to see these seven aspects of themselves, the client is finally on the path to effortlessness.

From *The Coaching Starter Kit* by CoachVille.com, published by W. W. Norton & Company, Inc.
Form courtesy of and copyrighted by Thomas Leonard

58 Things Clients Want Most

INDIVIDUALS

Make and keep more money
- Start saving/investing 10-30 percent of income
- Get a handle on spending, lifestyle, and habits
- Increase income by 20-200 percent
- Handle debt, financial problems, and crises
- Stabilize cash flow

Get more done in less time
- Get focused on what I most want to have
- Simplify my life, responsibilities, and projects
- Automate systems for peak efficiency
- Permanently eliminate inventory of to-do's
- Reduce the should's, could's, oughta's in life

Communicate much more effectively
- Say everything I need to; nothing withheld
- Motivate others more
- Respond better (by hearing it all)
- Be able to ask for what I want more
- Ask the right questions

Feel better physically and emotionally
- Get my home, office, car in perfect order
- Recognize and eliminate any high, hidden "life costs"
- Establish a reserve of time, space, money, and love
- Redesign eating and lifestyle habits
- Meet personal needs

Substantially increase quality of life
- Establish the perfect balance of home, work, and play
- Increase personal standards
- Strengthen professional network/personal community
- Have a whole lot more fun

Become closer with others
- Attract and deepen relationships with quality people
- Become more intimate with loved ones
- Learn to enjoy people more
- Know what I want for others

Eliminate the hassles of life
- Stop suffering, tolerating, waiting, and hoping
- Stop having problems
- Calm down; eliminate stress and accountability deferment tactics
- Resolve past matters, unfinished business
- Extend boundaries

Get on a path
- Develop my spiritual side/connection
- Discover personal mission, purpose, vision
- Reorient life exclusively around values
- Develop a stronger relationship with myself
- Be internally peaceful

BUSINESSES

Have a successful small business
- Start a new business
- Increase profitability by 20-500 percent
- Increase sales by 50-1,000 percent
- Develop a strategic and action plan
- Strengthen the internal management systems

Corporate work
- Build a cooperative culture of self-managing teams
- Establish a five- and twenty-year vision, mission, and strategy
- Train non-sales staff to sell, too
- Strategically reposition my business in markets/industry
- Double firm's sales volume and profitability

PROFESSIONALS
- Develop a full, successful practice
- Develop a strong reputation, be known as a model
- Manage clients better
- Increase sales and profitability
- Recognize and eliminate high, hidden delivery costs

COACHES
- Get trained and master the craft of coaching
- Develop a full, successful practice
- Grow through obstacles
- Obtain coach certification
- Develop a strong reputation; be known as a model

BENEFITS OF HAVING A COACH
- You'll reach for much, much more because of the support and structure the coach provides.
- You'll start making and keeping more money and get on the path to financial independence.
- You'll make better decisions because you can run your ideas by an objective listener.

From *The Coaching Starter Kit* by CoachVille.com, published by W. W. Norton & Company, Inc.

20 Things I Want for My Clients

1. To feel they're living a happier and more meaningful life

2. To have enough energy to easily get through their days

3. To have more than enough money to pay their bills on-time and still save for later

4. To have wonderful, fulfilling relationships with their relatives, spouses, children, and friends

5. To believe that they are successful

6. To live in a physical space that is pleasing and energizing

7. To feel joy every day

8. To work at something that feels good

9. To not have regrets

10. To spend quality time with themselves, alone

11. To develop and maintain friendships that give them great pleasure

12. To not be tolerating loads of things

13. To create boundaries that are healthy and protective

14. To attract opportunities easily

15. To have reserves of everything (time, money, love, confidence, etc.)

16. To pass along the joy they feel

17. To be a model for others

18. To live with integrity, without effort

19. To love easily and without limit

20. To live their best life

Coaching Strategies:
88 Ways to Help Your Clients Get More of What They Want

There are many different ways that a coach can support a client to reach his/her goals and achieve both success and happiness. Some of the strategies are known as front-door strategies, such as goal-setting, weekly coaching support, asking the right questions, making direct requests, and listening. Others are known as back-door strategies, meaning that they focus the client on something other than the goal itself.

Back-door coaching makes coaching powerful, easy, and sustainable. As a result of working in one of these back-door areas, the goal—or a better one—is reached, often in less time.

1. MODIFY GOALS
Most goals need fine-tuning
- Change the goal
- Clarify the goal
- Make the goal value-based
- Abandon a goal
- Abandon all goals/goals-free zone
- Simplify the goal
- Make the goal clearly measurable
- Eliminate pipe-dream goals
- Change measures of success
- Set tangible goals versus intangible ones

2. STRENGTHEN INTERNALLY
Strength permits rapid growth
- Resolve the past
- Extend boundaries
- Build character
- Improve self-esteem
- Increase self-confidence
- Restore integrity
- Exercise daily
- Maintain excellent eating habits
- Eliminate emotional stress/drain

3. IMPROVE ENVIRONMENT
Environments support and shape
- Establish support structure
- Establish daily routine/habits
- Expand professional network
- Create loving home environment
- Create productive work environment
- Acquire the right tools/equipment
- Live well but within means
- Resolve upsetting relationships/situations
- Reduce clutter, clean up physical spaces
- Focus on quality versus quantity

4. CREATE A GAP
Gaps pull a client forward
- Help client to discover a truth
- Help client to find their vision
- Point out a better paradigm
- Plant a seed
- Draw a distinction
- Focus on financial independence
- Focus on a perfect life
- Fuel desire/find hot button
- Set "impossible" goals
- Point out unseen options

5. USE A PROGRAM/CHECKLIST
Coach 24-hours-a-day with programs
- Coaching Focus Area
- Promise Log
- The Action Log
- Special Project

From *The Coaching Starter Kit* by CoachVille.com, published by W. W. Norton & Company, Inc.

6. BOND FULLY

Trust accelerates growth

- Listen to care, not to coach
- Identify with client's feelings/situation
- Validate client's concerns
- Share your insights/intuition
- Be deeply respectful of client
- Focus on client, not just the result
- Empathize, no matter what
- Find common ground
- Tell the truth, always; be forthright
- Remind the client who they are

7. CHALLENGE AND PUSH

We all need a push at times

- Speak with an edge
- Expect the client's best
- Make a direct request
- Correct assumptions
- Demand a change
- Be directive, instruct
- Illuminate a path/steps to follow
- Identify potential consequences
- Refuse to coach client on a certain topic

8. MAKE CLIENT SMARTER

Educate them continuously

- Package thoughts into messages
- Devise overarching/meta-strategies
- Increase client awareness of their evolution
- Share principles/maxims

- Tell stories/parables
- Recommend a book for client to read
- Ask the client to teach others

9. IMPROVE/STRENGTHEN

Help the client to build skills and self

- Communication skills
- Selling/Marketing skills
- Internet/Cyber skills
- Relationships/Networks
- Space/Freedom
- Talents/Skills
- Willingness/Flexibility
- Choices/Options
- Thinking process/Openness

10. REDUCE/ELIMINATE

Less creates space for more

- Tolerations
- Problems
- Compromise
- Resistance/Obstacles
- Procrastinating/Waiting/If . . .Then
- Personality/Emotional problems
- Doubt/Uncertainty
- Fear
- Stress
- Bad habits

From *The Coaching Starter Kit* by CoachVille.com, published by W. W. Norton & Company, Inc.

Coaching Mistakes to Avoid

Check the box if you are making that particular mistake.

1. WRONG FOCUS

- ❏ Focusing on the client's goal/achievement to the exclusion of the person
- ❏ Working on wants and needs when, in fact, the client has integrity issues
- ❏ Trying to help by sharing tips/techniques when, in fact, the client just needs to be heard
- ❏ Getting led down diversionary tunnels by your client because you can't see the real problem, opportunity, or situation
- ❏ Letting clients select goals that they have not had much luck with in the past
- ❏ Getting sidetracked by a client's personal problems
- ❏ Trying to push clients through obstacles instead of helping them fully understand the obstacle's dynamic
- ❏ Paying more attention to what the client is saying rather than to what their behavior is saying
- ❏ Letting clients set their coaching goals without your full consent
- ❏ Forcing a topic on which the client does not want to focus, even if you feel it really needs to be discussed

2. WEAK COACHING

- ❏ Passively coaching and responding during the coaching sessions instead of asking for more from the client
- ❏ Focusing on tactical matters or details when strategic coaching is needed, and vice-versa
- ❏ Being too nice/patient to the point where you are not saying what needs to be said
- ❏ Slipping into the role of motivator or "cattle-prodder" of your clients, instead of being their collaborative partner

- ❏ Working too hard to make your clients successful instead of inspiring/challenging your client to do so for themselves
- ❏ Not setting specific goals or focusing enough on performance (unless client wants a discovery-type focus)
- ❏ Not directly and immediately addressing the client's personality problems, communication flaws, bad attitude, or resistance
- ❏ Not knowing or asking the right question(s)
- ❏ Accepting what the client says at face value, without clarifying or asking for evidence
- ❏ Coaching clients as if they are all the same

3. COMMUNICATION FLAWS

- ❏ Using jargon instead of simple words
- ❏ Interrupting the client's words in your desire to help/save time
- ❏ Not interrupting a client who is rambling because you do not want to be rude
- ❏ Being blunt because you feel you are correct, and not being mindful enough of the possible impact on your client's feelings
- ❏ Using e-mail with clients without going out of your way to make sure you add extra warmth, encouragement, and respect
- ❏ Not being responsible for how you are being heard
- ❏ Not sharing the inklings you are having—positive or negative
- ❏ Using a patronizing tone with clients, relating to them as someone who needs what you have to say
- ❏ Not hearing the often subtle clues that a client always gives the coach about what is most important to them, and the changes that they really want to make
- ❏ Trying to teach a concept to the client instead of just taking a piece of the concept and showing the client how to use it in a specific situation

4. EGOCENTRICITY

- ❏ Forcing your views or agenda on the client in your eagerness to help
- ❏ Not asking enough of your client because you are afraid of pushing him/her too hard
- ❏ Not asking your client to do more than you would be willing to do in the same situation (do not hold a client to your limits)
- ❏ Forcing your client to adopt your life approach, principles, or beliefs
- ❏ Getting your emotional needs met via your clients
- ❏ Taking/needing credit for your clients' successes, even if you were instrumental in the process
- ❏ Thinking that your clients should do what you coach them to do because you are the coach
- ❏ Underestimating the client's strengths, willingness, resources, and resourcefulness
- ❏ Expecting more of the client than they are truly capable of because you see their potential
- ❏ Encouraging the client to step out and follow his/her heart or pursue a dream, before they are emotionally ready or financially secure/responsible

5. CLIENT MANAGEMENT

- ❏ Letting the client consistently pay late
- ❏ Trying to coach in a restaurant or other public venue
- ❏ Not charging enough/too much
- ❏ Assuming your clients are not evolving and thus falling behind their changing/emerging needs
- ❏ Not tightly managing every logistical aspect of your practice (billing, prompt call-backs, etc.)
- ❏ Getting into business with your clients without first ending the coaching relationship or having a very clear partnership agreement
- ❏ Assuming your practice will build quickly and quitting your day job with that expectation
- ❏ Telling the client about your personal life, successes, failures, or problems, unless done so in the direct interest of the client
- ❏ Letting coaching sessions run late or making the client call back

- ❏ Having call-waiting or background noise that the client can hear during the session

6. UNPROFESSIONAL COACHING PRACTICES

- ❏ Firing clients because they are not performing/succeeding
- ❏ Collecting a percentage/bonus based on the client's results
- ❏ Thinking your job is primarily to share useful information and advice (better to be a full, collaborative partner)
- ❏ Telling the client not to worry so much or being otherwise disrespectful
- ❏ Taking sides with your client against the client's employer, spouse, friend, or other person
- ❏ Getting emotionally invested in the outcome of your coaching
- ❏ Talking about a client to a third party, unless cleared to do so by the client
- ❏ Hanging on to an unsuitable/unproductive client for the money
- ❏ Fining clients who do not take their promised actions
- ❏ Pigeonholing the client as a type
- ❏ Coaching on a problem/subject that you do not know enough about, unless you first tell the client of your lack of experience, and this ignorance cannot hurt the client

7. MARKETING/NEW CLIENT SELECTION

- ❏ Over-promising results in any way, instead of under-promising/not promising anything
- ❏ Talking people into hiring a coach, instead of helping them to see or create the value of coaching for themselves
- ❏ Selling people on the value of coaching, instead of selling people first on themselves
- ❏ Working with the non-coachable client or a client who is not emotionally ready for coaching
- ❏ Coaching friends or family members
- ❏ Coaching clients who need you or coaching too much, thus creating dependency/pressure

From *The Coaching Starter Kit* by CoachVille.com, published by W.W. Norton & Company, Inc.

- Asking or pressuring current clients for referrals, instead of finding more professional ways to let them know you have time for more business
- Not spending enough time determining your clients' learning styles and ways of doing things
- Not knowing what to say or do when a potential client calls you as a result of a referral or web link
- Assuming someone knows in advance how to be a great/successful client

8. CLIENT RETENTION/COACHING FLOW

- Having even one bad client who is causing you stress
- Not continually planting seeds to help the client see the next objective/focus
- Not helping the client to see the connection between a recent success and the changes/evolution they have been making
- Assuming that your clients remember/know how much they have benefited from your coaching
- Not periodically asking your client to specify what to do differently/better so that they will better benefit from your coaching
- Not knowing exactly what the client feels you are contributing to the relationship/coaching process
- Taking on more clients than you have the intellectual/emotional space for (not just time for)
- Failing to inquire about why a client terminates the coaching relationship, and making improvements as a result
- Assuming that because you have made a commitment to the client, the client has made a commitment to you
- Not initiating or bringing up the themes/issues/foci from which your clients will likely benefit

9. ERRONEOUS ASSUMPTIONS

- Assuming that X (situation, issue, stress) is a problem for the client because it is or would be a problem in your life

- Assuming you can and should coach anyone, if they are ready, willing, and able
- Assuming that your clients want/are ready to be successful, just because they say they are
- Assuming that your clients want to/can hear your advice at any given point, even if what you have to say is really good
- Assuming your clients are just like you, and need the same advice or type of support that you would
- Assuming the client can get it quickly, instead of giving the client enough time to process/accept your suggestions
- Assuming shared standards and boundaries
- Assuming that you are a terrific coach and thus stopping your own learning process
- Assuming that you have to know everything about coaching before you can be a really effective coach

10. BAD ADVICE

- Telling the client what to do (rather than co-creating the plan/strategy)
- Giving only one suggestion/option of what could be done
- Giving the right advice at the wrong time
- Giving legal, psychological, or medical advice without a license
- Getting too personal with your client, even if you are close
- Referring clients to other professionals whose competency or services you are not adequately familiar with
- Using a one-solution-fits-all coaching approach for all clients
- Making recommendations without having all of the relevant information and knowing the needs of the client
- Telling the client what will probably happen as a result of them following your recommendation
- Giving advice to one client that worked for another client, without customizing it

The High, Hidden Costs of Coaching

There are about thirty costs—many subtle or hidden—of coaching. These must all be eliminated in order for the coach to have a successful and sustainable practice, and to qualify to be a master coach.

Y	N	**FOUNDATION: HOW SOLID IS YOUR RELATIONSHIP WITH THE CLIENT?**
❑	❑	Have you over-promised results?
❑	❑	Have you misrepresented your experience or expertise in a rush to get the client?
❑	❑	Has the client taken the Coachability Index test (see Chapter 9) and not passed?
❑	❑	Is this the wrong type of client you should be coaching at this point in your development?
❑	❑	Does your client blindly follow your advice?
❑	❑	Does this client bring out your worst?
❑	❑	Are you undercharging?
❑	❑	Did you accept too many, too few, too big, too small, or not specific-enough goals from your client?
❑	❑	Did you violate your boundaries by accepting call times outside your desired schedule?
❑	❑	Do you not have a coach yourself?
❑	❑	Does the client see you as a technician (consultant) or as a coach?

Y	N	**FLOW: HOW EASY IS IT TO COACH AND WORK WITH THE CLIENT?**
❑	❑	Is the client a complainer?
❑	❑	Does the client pay more than seven days late? (Enforce your rules.)
❑	❑	Does the client come to the call more than three minutes late?
❑	❑	Does the client question everything you say? (Some trust is essential.)
❑	❑	Does the client fight your suggestions, only to accept them later?
❑	❑	Does the client not give you credit when credit is due you?
❑	❑	Does the client blame you for advice that didn't work out? (Share the responsibility.)
❑	❑	Does the client keep breaking his/her word?
❑	❑	Does the client not take action?
❑	❑	Is the client full of excuses?
❑	❑	Does the client just use you to talk to? (They should ask for your opinion.)
❑	❑	Do you gossip about your clients?

N	Y	FUTURE: IS A FANTASTIC FUTURE BEING BUILT BETWEEN YOU?

(Questions phrased in the positive mode versus the negative tone of above questions. Notice new position of N and Y.)

N	Y	
❑	❑	Is this client on a solid, fast track?
❑	❑	Is this client going to be able to pay increasing fees?
❑	❑	Does this client keep you on your toes?
❑	❑	Does this client send you business?
❑	❑	Does this client make you an extraordinary coach?
❑	❑	Is this client full of projects and ideas for the future?
❑	❑	Does this client have their vision, purpose, and mission clearly defined?

_____   **TOTAL 2ⁿᵈ COLUMN BOXES CHECKED**

SCORING KEY

25–30   You are virtually cost-free and should have an effortless practice.

20–24   Pretty good; your practice should be moving along. Go for 30!

15–19   Not bad, but you are being dragged down by your clients.

0–14   Not good, you have an expensive practice—eliminate 5 costs, fast!

12 Reasons That Coaches Are Not As Successful As They Could Be

1. **You don't know exactly what you are selling**

   Ask your clients to describe exactly what you provide for them. Sell that.

2. **Your communication style or personality puts people off**

   We all come across in a particular way. Get the facts. They're crucial to know.

3. **You hold back some of what you see and sense**

   Clients want the three "I's" from you: your instincts, intuition, and inklings.

4. **You are using only a single model for your coaching**

   The market wants flexibility and customized solutions. Why use only one model?

5. **You need clients, and it shows**

   Keep your day job until you have a waiting list of clients. Fear is consuming.

6. **You try to sell coaching as a professional service**

   Coaching is boring. People don't buy boring. But they do buy a better life.

7. **You don't know how to market your talents**

   Every coach has something to offer. Get help in articulating your palette.

8. **You aren't hearing what your clients need, want, or are saying**

   Coaches lose clients because they aren't fully hearing exactly what's wanted.

9. **You aren't using the web as a key part of your marketing strategy**

   Ultimately, the best clients will come to you via e-marketing. Embrace it now.

10. **You feel you should be fully trained before you start coaching**

    Get formally trained, but also learn 90 percent of what you need from your clients.

11. **You haven't arranged for enough support or encouragement**

    Starting any business takes time, structure, and strategies. Invest in support.

12. **Maybe you are meant for another career or iteration of coaching**

    Sometimes, coaching is a stepping stone for another career or small business.

From *The Coaching Starter Kit* by CoachVille.com, published by W.W. Norton & Company, Inc.
Form courtesy of and copyrighted by Thomas Leonard

133

COMMUNICATING WITH THE CLIENT
90+ Common Communication Faults

What mistakes are you making when you open your mouth? Here are 100 common communication faults. Use this checklist when working with a client to strengthen their effectiveness, or as part of your own professional development.

1. LACK OF CREDIBILITY
- ❑ Over-promises results/benefits
- ❑ Overstates facts, hypes
- ❑ Lies, misrepresents; dishonest
- ❑ Sneaky, nor forthright
- ❑ Eager to please, needs approval
- ❑ Pretentious, tries to impress
- ❑ Sounds needy, desperate
- ❑ Insincere-sounding, not real
- ❑ Justifies, over-explains

2. DISRESPECTFUL
- ❑ Critical, harsh, judgmental
- ❑ Insensitive, no compassion
- ❑ One-ups, downplays efforts
- ❑ Ignores what was said
- ❑ Patronizes
- ❑ Sexist, bigoted, intolerant
- ❑ Digs, undermines
- ❑ Inappropriate comments, humor
- ❑ Stingy with praise or support
- ❑ Hard-sell, tries to convince, trick

3. DISRUPTS FLOW
- ❑ Too positive, pushes mood
- ❑ Too fast, adrenalized
- ❑ Inattentive, easily distracted
- ❑ Information-reactive (responds only to information, not person/feelings)
- ❑ Literal, can't get gist easily
- ❑ Rehashes the point
- ❑ Responds with non-sequiturs
- ❑ Interrogates
- ❑ Overly concerned

4. LACK OF CLARITY
- ❑ Trite, boring, old, useless
- ❑ Clichéd answers/quotes
- ❑ Confusing, overly complicated
- ❑ Vague, rambling, repetitive
- ❑ Mishears, mislabels, assumes
- ❑ Consumes info vs. assimilates info
- ❑ Dogmatic, righteous, singular
- ❑ Linear, 2D, flat information
- ❑ Too much information
- ❑ Too quick with advice

5. NO WARMTH
- ❑ Cold, icy
- ❑ No personality, flat, no fizz
- ❑ Measured, controlled
- ❑ Suspicious, distrusting
- ❑ Negative, jaded, acerbic
- ❑ Quickly points out flaws
- ❑ Rigid
- ❑ Highly technical language
- ❑ Analytical, logic-without-feelings
- ❑ Judges, labels, compartmentalizes

6. WEAK LISTENER
- ❑ Listens too hard
- ❑ Listens only for the familiar

From *The Coaching Starter Kit* by CoachVille.com, published by W. W. Norton & Company, Inc.
Form courtesy of and copyrighted by Thomas Leonard

❑ Can't multi-process (can only hear one idea/subject/problem at a time)

❑ Listens blindly (not sure what to listen for)

❑ No echo (speaker doesn't feel heard)

❑ Always preparing a response; misses what is being said

❑ Reacts negatively, stops listening

❑ Interrupts too much

❑ Corrects too much

7. POOR SPEAKER

❑ Doesn't condition or contextualize

❑ Uses jargon

❑ Uses generic, non-specific language

❑ Has inadequate vocabulary

❑ Doesn't know distinctions

❑ Ignorant, uniformed about subject

❑ "I/me" oriented

❑ Oblivious of people's reactions

❑ Numb, unaware of own feelings

❑ Steps over/ignores key clues

8. WRONG FOCUS

❑ Symptoms-oriented (vs. source)

❑ Problem-oriented (vs. source)

❑ Past-oriented (vs. present)

❑ Future-oriented (vs. present)

❑ Consequence-oriented (vs. cause)

❑ Old-fashioned (vs. current thinking)

❑ Hearsay, gossip (vs. fact)

❑ Theoretical (vs. practical)

❑ Tactical (vs. strategic)

9. INEFFECTIVE STYLE

❑ Oblique, hinting (vs. direct)

❑ Slow, plodding (vs. quick)

❑ Draining (consumes space/energy)

❑ Coaching vs. consulting

❑ Coaching vs. helping

❑ Intense, over-eager, too "on"

❑ Bossy, domineering, controlling

❑ Sugar-coated

❑ Broadcasts, lectures, speaks "at"

❑ Talks more than listens

10. ANNOYING VOICE/TONE

❑ Feeble, weak, doesn't reach/affect

❑ Loud, booming, overpowering

❑ Nasal, grating

❑ High pitched, squeaky

❑ Hesitant, tentative, unsure

❑ Whiney

❑ Negative tone

❑ Heavy, significant, overacting

What to Say to Your Client:
Helpful Phrases and Questions to Share

1. ENCOURAGEMENT

- You're doing great! Keep going.
- You've got what it takes.
- Stick with it, especially now.
- Don't even think about giving up.
- I believe in you and your ability to reach this goal.
- It will get better!
- Whenever you try something new, surprises happen.
- I am here for you.
- Don't listen much to the naysayers.
- Whose opinion matters most to you?

2. EMPATHY

- I know exactly how you feel.
- I am so sorry to hear that.
- It must be frustrating.
- That's terrible news!
- How are you handling that?
- How are you feeling right now?
- What would you like to hear right now?
- We'll get through this.
- When is the last time you were this challenged?
- How can I help?

3. CHALLENGE

- Your attitude could use improvement.
- When will you reach the goal?
- Try doing it this way.
- You are not being responsible.
- This situation is not okay with me, as your coach.
- Stop doing that!
- Why is that happening, do you think?
- You need to face this head on.

- Make this your first priority.
- You can do better than that.

4. CLARIFICATION

- Where did you learn that?
- What is the truth in this situation?
- Why is this happening to you?
- How do you know that for sure?
- Why do you sound surprised by this?
- How long has this been going on?
- What's most important to you right now?
- Is that a need or a want?
- What's the worst part of the situation?
- What's the source of the problem?

5. REFOCUS

- Why won't you let go of this?
- Let's focus on what is working.
- You have special skills that can be developed.
- Let's change the focus.
- You're stuck on this goal; let's find a better one.
- What do you want most?
- Which of your resources isn't fully utilized?
- Assume the worst. Now what?
- Assuming life is perfect, what's the lesson?
- What's an easier approach to take?

6. STRENGTHENING

- Is this solvable?
- Fixing your cash flow is the first priority.
- Your integrity is weak.
- You sound tired.
- Your boundaries are weak.
- What's your primary character flaw?

From *The Coaching Starter Kit* by CoachVille.com, published by W. W. Norton & Company, Inc.
Form courtesy of and copyrighted by Thomas Leonard

- Let's work on your selling skills.
- Do you know how you come across?
- Your standards are too low.

7. PERSONAL DEVELOPMENT

- Let's work on the Action/Promise Log
- What are your values?
- How strong is your personal foundation?
- Let's build up what you have.
- You need more space, not time.
- What gives you pleasure?
- Simplify your life.

8. EXPANDING

- Are you up to this?
- What is your vision?
- Describe your ideal life to me.
- What motivates you in general?
- You need to think a lot bigger.
- How would an expert handle this problem?
- You need a clear strategy.
- What's the ultimate outcome?
- What kind of person do you want to be?

9. EVOKE

- Tell me more about that.
- What are the options here?
- If there was a solution, what would it be?
- Snap out of it.
- Why are you so rigid and resistant?

- How do I reach you?
- Why are you tolerating that?
- What part of you needs to be reached?
- Tell me what to do.
- There's a truth that needs to be said.

10. ACTION

- What's the first step to take?
- Are you ready to get to work?
- Hang up, do that, and call me back in twenty minutes. What's next?
- What's the single daily action to take?
- What should you stop doing?
- What do you need?
- Who can you ask for help?
- What's the most pivotal thing you can do?
- What will you get done in the next hour?
- How can I coach you even more effectively?

From *The Coaching Starter Kit* by CoachVille.com, published by W. W. Norton & Company, Inc. Form courtesy of and copyrighted by Thomas Leonard

95 Creative and Powerful Ways to Make Your Point

1. RELEVANT
Make your point personal.

- Ask open-ended questions
- Orient around listener's culture
- Point to recent events
- Offer a real-life example
- Link to a current trend
- Refer to a movie, song, or ad
- Link to a commonly-held belief
- Share a personal experience
- Emotionalize the point
- Mention someone they know

2. COMPELLING
Make your point.

- Point out consequences
- Offer a conundrum
- Show cause and effect
- Tap into a source of fear
- Make a bold, evocative statement
- Provide a needed solution
- Ask a premise-shaking question
- Describe before and after states
- Introduce a better paradigm
- Offer a new thought or idea

3. BENEFICIAL
Show how the listener can:

- Make more money
- Have more time
- Experience more happiness
- Feel younger

- Gain a competitive advantage
- Reduce a financial cost
- Have more love
- Reduce emotional stress
- Get more leverage

4. COMPREHENSIBLE
Make your point easy to understand.

- Draw a distinction
- Share an anecdote
- Use a symbol or quote
- Craft a metaphor
- Identify a simile
- Describe a vivid image
- Use a formula
- Foster a spirited discussion
- Provide a demonstration

5. CREDIBLE
Prove the point; make it believable.

- Identify examples in nature
- Quote a fact or statistic
- Identify a universal truth
- Describe a related historical event
- Show how the point is part of a bigger system
- Relate to a well-known person
- Outline point's source/provenance
- Link to a physical or natural law
- Mention related current research
- Help people want to learn the point

From *The Coaching Starter Kit* by CoachVille.com, published by W. W. Norton & Company, Inc.

139

6. ENTERTAINING

Help people want to learn the point.

- Take an unconventional approach
- Identify the meta-message
- Use multimedia (video, music, etc.)
- Share a dramatic, yet true, story
- Give permission/foster acceptance
- Have/share your vision in the area
- Use humor; be funny, witty, quick
- Point out an absurdity of life
- Use a prop to make your point
- Share a success story

7. ASSIMILATIVE

Help people to integrate the point.

- Role play with the audience
- Custom fit your information
- Give readers an exercise to do
- Get people to share their views
- Debrief/summarize what was said
- Ask listener to further develop point
- Ask listener to apply/use the point
- Describe the shift that is possible
- Suggest what to stop doing
- Inform listener about physical reactions

8. USEFUL AND PRACTICAL

Show people how to use your point.

- Provide action steps
- Identify unspoken objections
- Point out easily-missed fallacies
- Explain implementation strategy
- Identify/remove blocks to implementation
- Correct false assumptions
- Show how to use point with others
- Inform listeners of possible reactions with use
- Give fieldwork/homework

9. MOTIVATING

Get people excited about your point.

- Package point into a catchphrase
- Ask a close-ended question
- Make a direct request
- Point out what's possible
- Suggest a life reorientation
- Create urgency
- Have a passion for your point
- Present/identify a related toleration
- Validate listener's experience/views

10. MEMORABLE

Make it easy to remember the point.

- Phrase point as a maxim
- Create an acronym
- Share your opinion
- Package your point as a life lesson
- Repeat your point in different ways
- Provide a model/example of use
- Illustrate your point using a Venn diagram
- Describe smell/color/texture
- Create/relate to a slogan/jingle
- Evolve the point while sharing it

90+ Things a Coach Listens for and Hears

1. DISSONANCE/CONFUSION

- Words don't match actions
- Tone of voice doesn't match words
- Inability to identify/share feelings
- No or slow progress
- Easy steps not taken
- Resistance to support
- Reliance on clichés, jargon
- Attracting continual problems
- Playing dumb/dependent

2. DESIRE/READINESS

- Excitement
- Willingness
- Eagerness to start
- Flowing of ideas
- Self-motivation
- Exciting dreams
- Faster-than-expected performance
- Serendipity
- Synchronicity

3. RESOURCES/ASSETS

- Inner strength
- Unknown skills/talents
- Size/power of network
- Past experience/expertise
- Resourcefulness
- Specialized knowledge
- Special way of thinking
- Communication/selling skills
- Strong reputation

4. FEARS/DOUBTS

- Sharp intake of breath
- Shortened breathing
- Too many questions
- Saying yes but meaning no
- Talking slowly
- Procrastination
- Nervousness in voice
- Pulling away from coach
- Diverting away from goal
- Changing subject

5. DEVELOPMENTAL LEVEL

- Strength of personal foundation
- Knowledge of attraction principles
- Personal maturity/self-responsibility
- Flexibility
- Response time to unexpected problems
- High standards
- Strong character
- Adequate reserves
- Ability to think conceptually
- Type of emotional reactions

6. COACH'S REACTIONS

- Frustration
- Resentment/anger
- Envy
- Strong desire to help
- Strong desire to protect
- Confusion
- Holding back
- Pushing the client
- Resignation

From *The Coaching Starter Kit* by CoachVille.com, published by W. W. Norton & Company, Inc.

7. PERSONAL QUALITIES

- Honesty
- Honor
- Responsibility
- Respectfulness
- Accountability
- Generosity
- Maturity
- Initiative
- Caring
- Strength

8. QUALITY OF RELATIONSHIPS

- Children
- Spouse
- Parents/Family
- Friends
- Acquaintances/Neighbors
- Co-workers/Colleagues
- Vendors/Service
- Mentors/Teachers
- Clients/Customers
- Yourself

9. QUALITY OF LIFE

- Tolerations
- Self-care
- Commitments
- Goals
- Problems/Struggles
- Work/Home environment
- Stress

- Desires/Needs
- Pace

10. MIND/INTELLECT

- Quickness
- Intuitive ability
- Type of learner
- Opinions
- General knowledge
- Beliefs
- Expectations in life
- Reactions to life
- Ability to process logically
- Cultural restrictions/blocks

Words That Encourage/Discourage

Encouragement is valuing and accepting people as they really are (not putting conditions on acceptance); pointing out the positive aspect of behavior; showing faith in people so that they can come to believe in themselves; recognizing effort and improvement (rather than requiring achievement); and showing appreciation for contributions. Accepting people as they are encourages growth by increasing their sense of worth and confidence. Reminding people that there is always more to attain tends to discourage them and make them feel inadequate.

WORDS THAT ENCOURAGE

- Everybody makes mistakes.
- You're the kind who can do it.
- You certainly are improving.
- Mistakes do happen.
- I like the way you are listening.
- Give it a try. You can do it.
- That is very nice work.
- Thanks so very much.
- I'm glad you enjoy listening.
- It sounds like you enjoyed that.
- How do you feel about it?
- Knowing you, I'm sure you'll do fine.
- I have a lot of confidence in you.
- It was very thoughtful of you to _____.
- Thanks, I really appreciate _____, because it makes my job easier.
- You're very good at _____. Would you do that for us?
- It looks as if you really worked hard on that.
- It looks as if you spent a lot of time thinking that through.
- I see that you're moving along.
- Look at the progress you've made.
- You may not feel you've reached your goal, but look how far you've come.
- I like you.
- That is really great.
- I appreciate your cooperative behavior.

- It's so nice to know someone like you.
- Keep up your good work.
- What a neat idea!
- I've never thought of that.
- I really appreciate your help.
- I know, it's really hard.
- I like the way you handled that.
- I'm glad you are pleased with it.

WORDS THAT DISCOURAGE

- I'm ready to give up on you.
- You can't do anything right.
- Look at all those mistakes.
- That's good, but…
- You are so clumsy.
- Here, let me do it for you.
- No, do it this way.
- _____ can do it. Why can't you?
- I've told you a thousand times.
- When are you going to grow up?
- I told you that would happen.
- Why don't you ever listen?
- You have rocks in your head.
- Why are you always so slow?
- Everybody knows that.
- Boys don't cry.
- Now, you aren't hurt.
- You are nothing but a bully, liar, cheat, etc.
- You are wrong.
- What am I going to do with you?
- What are you, a sissy?
- You are driving me crazy.
- Lazy.
- I knew you wouldn't do it.
- You never pay attention.
- You don't know how to do that.
- Why don't you think?
- That's good, but I'm sure you can do better next time.
- You do not have a reason to feel that way.

From *The Coaching Starter Kit* by CoachVille.com, published by W. W. Norton & Company, Inc.
Form courtesy of and copyrighted by FEC Enterprises, Inc.

Confrontation

Take the following steps when making a confrontation.

1. If the person changes the subject, say, "Please answer my question, then we can talk about the new subject."

2. If the person answers only part of the question, ask him/her to complete the answer.

3. Ask the person if he/she is aware that he/she didn't answer the original question, then ask the original question again.

4. Ask the same question again, using exactly the same words and tone of voice.

5. Say, "Maybe I didn't make the question clear," and ask it again, clarifying if necessary.

6. If the person answers with a long story, interrupt the story and ask, "How is this an answer to my question?" You may have to ask the person if he/she remembers the original question. If he/she doesn't, repeat it.

7. If the person cries, shouts, or demonstrates some other extreme behavior, deal with it as appropriate, then decide whether to go back to the original question.

8. Give the person permission to say out loud, "I won't answer your question."

From *The Coaching Starter Kit* by CoachVille.com, published by W. W. Norton & Company, Inc.
Form courtesy of and copyrighted by Jon Weiss, Ph. D. and Laurie Weiss, Ph. D.

Chapter 5

Practice Upkeep

ORGANIZING YOUR SESSIONS
Monthly Practice Checklist

Stay ahead of your clients and on top of your practice with this list. Color in the boxes as you complete each step, each month. Customize to suit your needs.

ACTION	J	F	M	A	M	J	J	A	S	O	N	D
Send birthday and holiday cards.												
Send progress reports.												
Identify three things you want for each client next month.												
Send/call with an acknowledgment for each client's growth.												
Collect all receivables.												
Prepare your monthly financial statement.												
Market until your practice is full.												
Schedule speaking engagements or workshops and enroll your clients.												
Buy more supplies or new equipment to do a great job.												
Send billing out.												
Pay your own bills, early.												
Make appropriate policy or pricing changes for the practice.												
Follow up with all leads and referrals.												
Ask for at least five referrals from current clients.												
Take plenty of time off.												
Update your Action Log, Special Project, and other programs.												

Monthly Coaching Form

Please fill in and fax the form to your coach, or use the headings as the basis for an e-mail.

Client name: _____   Coach name: _____

Client ph/fax: _____   Coach ph/fax: _____

BACKGROUND/OVERALL GOALS TO KEEP IN MIND

1. _____

2. _____

3. _____

HOW WILL YOU KNOW THAT YOUR COACHING HAS BEEN SUCCESSFUL THIS MONTH?

1. _____

2. _____

3. _____

WEEK 1—DATE/TIME:

To celebrate

_____

_____

To discuss

_____

_____

To do by next week

_____

_____

WEEK 2—DATE/TIME:

To celebrate

_____

_____

To discuss

_____

_____

To do by next week

_____

_____

WEEK 3—DATE/TIME:

To celebrate

_____

_____

To discuss

_____

_____

To do by next week

_____

_____

WEEK 4—DATE/TIME:

To celebrate

_____

_____

To discuss

_____

_____

To do by next week

_____

_____

How successful was your coaching this month? ____ /out of 10. Why?

_____

Coaching Session Agenda

Use this master checklist to make sure you are doing a complete job. Fill in the first section prior to the call. Use this form during the session to document the client's activity and the content of the call.

Client _____

Date _____ Time _____

BEFORE THE CALL

❏ Review the previous call.

❏ Review this client's file, promise log, and goal list, and outline what you want to accomplish/discuss now:

1. _____

2. _____

3. _____

4. _____

STARTING THE CALL

❏ _____, how are you? I am glad you called.

❏ Tell me what's happened since our last call.

Shifts _____

Results/wins _____

Problems _____

Progress report _____

CONTENT OF THE CALL

❏ Distinction shared _____

❏ Requests made _____

❏ Observations shared _____

❏ Advice given _____

❏ _____

❏ _____

TOWARDS THE END OF THE CALL

❏ _____, we have about 5 minutes left.

❏ Homework given _____

❏ Confirm next call date, time and procedure.

AFTER THE CALL

❏ Update client's file and file this form.

From *The Coaching Starter Kit* by CoachVille.com, published by W. W. Norton & Company, Inc.

FILLING YOUR PRACTICE

100+ Ways to Fill Your Practice (and Keep it Full)

1. Give your service away for free

2. Give your services away for free to three clients who can fill your practice

3. Lead a workshop for your current clients and don't charge them for it

4. Lead a workshop for your friends, clients, prospects, and the public for a very affordable tuition

5. Ask five clients for five referrals each

6. Host a weekly luncheon or monthly party

7. Tell clients that their referrals are one of the ways you are paid

8. Join three clubs or organizations where your ideal clients would likely be members

9. Deliver a measurable 20 percent more than what your average client expects

10. Open an office that inspires you to do your best work

11. Offer to help three people in trouble who cannot afford your fee

12. Become a known resource by having or getting to know fifty highly qualified people who provide services that your ideal clients need

13. Orient at least 25 percent of your practice around your special talent

14. Host gatherings of your competitors

15. Train your clients how to speak about you

16. Become known as unconditionally constructive

17. Write an article on something new in your profession

18. Mentor an apprentice coach

19. Hire an appointment setter

20. Know and articulate your three basic messages

21. Tell people the ten things that you want for them

22. Set your practice standards high and honor them

23. Send out a monthly newsletter

24. Send out a monthly practice letter

25. Speak to groups at least once per week

26. Send birthday and holiday cards to your clients

27. Write a book that breaks the rules

28. Send "Request Letters" to colleagues

29. Become known for three special things, but deliver all you can until your practice is full

30. Invest 10 percent of your revenue in training, coaching, and development

31. Dress professionally

32. Know your vision and be able to share it

33. Establish yourself as a center of influence

34. Deepen your relationship with ten centers of influence

35. Raise your fees

36. Meet your personal needs outside of your practice

37. Give a thank-you gift for each referral

38. Master the skill of converting leads into clients

39. Immediately acknowledge a referral

40. Do not offer your business card; rather, ask for permission to call

41. Ask, don't plead, for more business—but do ask

42. Be more interested than interesting

43. Underpromise, but get the client anyway

44. Handle everything fully

45. Package promotional materials to stun people

46. Have something worthwhile to say

47. Have referrals call you; don't chase them

48. Do more work for current clients

49. Know what services you cannot or will not offer

50. Expect a lot from your clients

51. Package your services to create an annuity stream

52. Upgrade your clientele
53. Drastically cut business and personal expenses to be 25 percent more profitable right now
54. Get more permission than you'll ever need from everyone
55. Be coached
56. Speak in terms of benefits, not features
57. Speak in second person (you), not first person (I)
58. Take the initiative; don't wait
59. Don't gossip
60. Put the relationship ahead of the result
61. Value your time
62. Don't hide behind a brochure
63. Advance your profession
64. Take a vacation each quarter
65. Have something to look forward to each evening
66. Be straightforward, but don't spill your guts
67. Offer to help when you can do so, without such help "costing" you
68. Know exactly what you can do for others and let them know it
69. Invite key people out
70. Tell people what you want them to do
71. Be selective of prospective clients
72. Take rejection gracefully
73. Be fully caught up
74. Have time slots open, blank files prepared, and welcome packets printed
75. Under-inform instead of over-inform
76. Anticipate and respond to client needs and concerns
77. Use a written agreement in all cases
78. Budget 5 percent for advertising, gifts, and referral source management

79. Value each client as a key asset: a ten-year revenue stream
80. Decide to become attraction- vs promotion-based
81. Co-design work to be performed; let the client contribute to your success
82. Think holistically, act specifically
83. Align your goals with your values
84. Interest your clients to send you clients
85. If people have not been referred to you, find out why
86. Make a list of your top ten clients and who sent them to you (The Referral Tree)
87. Introduce yourself in ten words or less
88. Know what would make you irresistible to your ideal clientele
89. Serve, don't sell
90. Eliminate distractions
91. Have 50 percent more business than you need
92. Identify the 20 percent of your clients who can bring you the other 80 percent through referrals
93. Believe in your work
94. Be responsible for how you are heard, not just what you say
95. Deliver the message; and then let people choose
96. Fully inform, don't hold back from your clients
97. Have a self-introduction that engages people
98. Meet with your personal group of advisors weekly
99. Write at least one acknowledgment note per day
100. Value your time at $100-$300 per hour
101. Save at least 10 percent of your income
102. Make one unscheduled call to a client each day

From *The Coaching Starter Kit* by CoachVille.com, published by W.W. Norton & Company, Inc. Form courtesy of and copyrighted by Thomas Leonard

More on Filling Your Practice

This list contains steps and suggestions to help you fill your coaching practice. Some of the suggestions will help you to become a better marketer, others will help you improve your networking, positioning, and revenue-enhancing strategies. And some are quality-of-life improvement suggestions that will help you become more attractive to yourself and to others.

1. PUBLIC RELATIONS

Become known locally/nationally.

- Hire a PR firm
- Write a column for local newspaper
- Appear on TV talk shows
- Speak on radio talk shows
- Be quoted as an expert
- Send out press releases
- Identify global need/link to coaching
- Do something newsworthy
- Offer free coaching to high profile clients
- Develop a press kit

2. ELECTRONIC MARKETING

Become Internet-marketing savvy.

- Develop a professional website of useful content
- Add meta tags for search engines
- Link site to Internet search engines
- Link site to/from other coaches
- Add yourself to coach referral.com
- Create a weekly e-advice letter
- Create and broadcast tips
- Ask for input from subscribers
- Get links from other sites

3. PERSONAL MARKETING

Develop an extensive network.

- Build a research and development team
- Get to know top coaches
- Distribute a newsletter 4 times/year
- Join/form an alliance of coaches
- Improve your personality/style
- Become someone worth knowing
- Host soireés/groups in your home
- Offer to help people as a habit

4. REPUTATION/CREDIBILITY

Become respected as a coach.

- Develop several specialties
- Obtain appropriate training and certification
- Develop an edge
- Offer to teach for other coaches
- Take a poll/publish a report
- Join the International Coach Federation
- Write a book
- Write magazine articles

5. PROFESSIONAL DEVELOPMENT

Become an expert at what you do.

- Develop listening skills
- Develop diagnostic skills
- Speak simply and jargon-free
- Know your coaching skills
- Know one-hundred key distinctions (i.e. what is urgent and important)

From *The Coaching Starter Kit* by CoachVille.com, published by W. W. Norton & Company, Inc.

157

- Read important magazines
- Develop strong and savvy opinions
- Develop lasering skills
- Attend coaching conferences

6. SALES SKILLS

Know how to sell really, really well.

- Create a one sentence self-introduction
- Develop sales lines
- Know what you're selling
- Be fearless; ask for the order
- Develop conversion language
- Discern what's wanted/needed
- Ask open-ended questions
- Get to know the person/buyer
- Find a way to serve every buyer
- Tell buyers about themselves

7. CLIENT REFERRALS

Become highly referable.

- Know your coaching strengths
- Know where you need to improve
- Let clients know you have room
- Ask clients for referrals
- Offer free introductory services
- Help clients to really succeed
- Challenge current clients
- Identify your ideal client type
- Let clients go who aren't right
- Specialize

8. PRODUCT/SERVICES

Give everyone something to buy.

- Offer free audio tapes
- Develop/sell an audio tape series
- Lead local workshops
- License your programs and work
- Offer result-specific coaching
- Offer industry-specific coaching
- Offer client-type coaching
- Offer group coaching
- Teach four- to twelve-week TeleClasses
- Launch a virtual university on the web

9. MARKETING TOOLS

Give people a chance to experience you.

- Offer free TeleClasses
- Offer free local workshops
- Distribute a printed brochure
- Give away one-hundred point checklists
- Give away free audio tapes
- Offer free coaching
- Offer free call-in days
- Develop/distribute a questionnaire
- Host weekly telephone discussions
- Host a virtual community

From *The Coaching Starter Kit* by CoachVille.com, published by W.W. Norton & Company, Inc.

FINANCIAL PLANNING

Checks Received

Read and complete the following.

DATE	$ FROM	FOR	COMMENTS

Total Checks Received This Month $

Cash Receipts Log

Use this form to keep track of the money you receive. Write down every check or cash you receive on this form before depositing. If you deposit several items together, use a separate line for each check and summarize the total so you can match up your deposits on the bank statement. Always fill in the amount column and categorize the nature of the income, using one or more of the five columns on the right. Use categories like coaching, seminars, public presentations, publications, sales, bonuses, and gifts. At the end of the month, quarter, or year, add up all of the columns to see how much money you received and how you earned it.

DATE	FROM	FOR	AMOUNT	TYPE OF INCOME				
			$					
			$					
			$					
			$					
			$					
			$					
			$					
			$					
			$					
			$					
			$					
			$					
			$					
			$					
			$					
Total This Page $								

From *The Coaching Starter Kit* by CoachVille.com, published by W. W. Norton & Company, Inc.

161

Current Top 20 Clients

Complete the following chart.

	NAME OF CLIENT	POTENTIAL INCOME FROM 90 DAYS OF COACHING
1.		
2.		
3.		
4.		
5.		
6.		
7.		
8.		
9.		
10.		
11.		
12.		
13.		
14.		
15.		
16.		
17.		
18.		
19.		
20.		
	TOTAL: $	

From *The Coaching Starter Kit* by CoachVille.com, published by W. W. Norton & Company, Inc.

Form courtesy of and copyrighted by Chris Barrow, Coach

163

Chapter 6

Niche Coaching

TYPES OF COACHING
100 Areas of Specialty

As the demand for coaching grows, so does the demand for coaching specialties. Below is a list of coaching specialties, many of which have already become popular. So, whether you are a coach-in-training wondering what the specialty options are, or a client seeking a specialist, the following list should be very useful.

Note: Some specialties require special licensing/testing by states or countries; others require advanced training, qualifications, and testing. Finally, some specialties are just now becoming popular.

1. CORPORATE

- ❏ Corporate coach
- ❏ Executive/CEO coach
- ❏ Organizational development coach
- ❏ Management coach
- ❏ Culture/Paradigm shift coach
- ❏ Leadership coach
- ❏ Board of Directors' coach
- ❏ Human resource coach
- ❏ Quality management coach
- ❏ Staff/Employee coach

2. MARKETING/SALES

- ❏ Sales coach
- ❏ Public relations coach
- ❏ Marketing coach
- ❏ Brand management coach
- ❏ Promotions coach
- ❏ Pricing strategy coach
- ❏ Buzz-development coach
- ❏ Advertising coach
- ❏ Direct marketing coach
- ❏ Personal marketing coach

3. SMALL BUSINESS

- ❏ New business coach
- ❏ Entrepreneur coach
- ❏ Business turnaround coach
- ❏ Multilevel marketing/Network marketing coach
- ❏ Networking coach
- ❏ Budgeting/Planning coach
- ❏ Business financial coach
- ❏ Mission development coach
- ❏ Marketing coach
- ❏ Partner's coach

4. RELATIONSHIPS

- ❏ Marriage coach
- ❏ Family coach
- ❏ Romance coach
- ❏ Team coach
- ❏ Parent coach
- ❏ Love coach
- ❏ Divorce recovery coach
- ❏ Couples coach
- ❏ Network development coach
- ❏ Intimacy coach

5. LIFESTAGE/LIFESTYLE

- ❏ Fresh start coach
- ❏ Generation X coach
- ❏ Baby boomer coach
- ❏ Retirement coach
- ❏ Lifestyle design coach
- ❏ Teen coach
- ❏ Student coach
- ❏ Workaholics coach
- ❏ Transition coach
- ❏ Personal turnaround coach

From *The Coaching Starter Kit* by CoachVille.com, published by W.W. Norton & Company, Inc.
Form courtesy of and copyrighted by Thomas Leonard, Coach U

6. QUALITY OF LIFE

- ❑ Nutrition/Diet coach
- ❑ Exercise/Fitness coach
- ❑ Vegan/Vegetarian coach
- ❑ Recreation coach
- ❑ Travel/Adventure coach
- ❑ Wellness coach
- ❑ Energy/Reiki coach
- ❑ Makeover coach
- ❑ Style coach
- ❑ Stress reduction coach

7. SUCCESS COACH

- ❑ Motivation/Edge coach
- ❑ Goals/Results coach
- ❑ Idea/Creativity coach
- ❑ Problem-solving/Solution coach
- ❑ Time management/Leverage coach
- ❑ Strategic coach
- ❑ Attraction coach
- ❑ Financial/Money coach
- ❑ Career coach
- ❑ Legacy/Achievement coach

8. SPECIAL MARKETS

- ❑ Consultants/Coaches coach
- ❑ MDs/Health Professional/Dental coach
- ❑ Attorney/Law firm coach
- ❑ CPA/Financial service coach
- ❑ Trainers/Speakers coach
- ❑ Gay/Lesbian coach
- ❑ Single mom/Parents coach
- ❑ Realtors/Real estate coach
- ❑ Therapists/Counselors coach
- ❑ Ministers/Caregivers coach

9. PERSONAL DEVELOPMENT

- ❑ 12-step/Recovery/Addiction coach
- ❑ Personal Foundation coach
- ❑ Integrity coach
- ❑ Balance coach
- ❑ Codependency coach
- ❑ Fear coach
- ❑ Post-12-step coach
- ❑ Resolution coach
- ❑ Attainments coach
- ❑ Spiritual coach

10. SPECIAL SKILLS AND SITUATIONS

- ❑ Communication coach
- ❑ Cyber coach
- ❑ Internet/Web coach
- ❑ Diagnostic coach
- ❑ Futurist coach
- ❑ Language/Phrasing coach
- ❑ Software/Computer coach
- ❑ Writing coach
- ❑ Personal organization coach
- ❑ General practitioner coach

The following two forms will help you, as a client of a business coach, to make money, although it may be your primary mission to make money at any cost. Mission doesn't necessarily refer to a charitable purpose for being in business; rather, your business mission is a way to share who you are and why you are devoting this stage of your life to this endeavor.

List the three products or services you or your firm offers of which you are most proud. _____

_____

_____

_____

Why are you so proud? Be specific. _____

_____

_____

_____

If every person in the world had access to these products or services, what difference would that make to our civilization? _____

_____

_____

_____

To individuals?_____

_____

_____

_____

Without access to your product or services, how do people suffer or what opportunities do they miss out on?

_____

_____

_____

If you had the resources, what single product or service would you spend your life making sure as many people as possible had access to? _____

_____

_____

_____

Why do you care so much about this product or service? What is your Business Mission Statement? _____

_____

_____

_____

Business Mission Statement #2

Ask yourself:

Why are we in this business?_____

_____

_____

_____

Who do we serve?_____

_____

_____

_____

What do we provide? _____

_____

_____

_____

What makes us and our products special? _____

_____

_____

_____

What are our goals?_____

_____

_____

_____

How do we know we are succeeding? _____

_____

_____

_____

From *The Coaching Starter Kit* by CoachVille.com, published by W. W. Norton & Company, Inc.
Form courtesy of and copyrighted by Thomas Leonard

10 Things I Want for My Business Clients

1. To have a clear financial and structural picture of where they've been, where they are currently, and where they want to go.

2. To work "on" their business instead of "in" it.

3. To be profitable from day one.

4. To run their business with integrity.

5. To have the proper help to run their business efficiently and profitably.

6. To be informed about what is going on in their industry.

7. To have their business succeed beyond their plans, and to be more profitable than they've budgeted for.

8. To attract customers without having to apply a great amount of effort.

9. To have a great life, too.

10. To have them get pleasure from their business tasks and duties.

From *The Coaching Starter Kit* by CoachVille.com, published by W.W. Norton & Company, Inc.
© Copyright 2002 by Kerul Kassel, New Leaf Systems

Business Plan: 1-Year Projection

INCOME	JAN	FEB	MAR	APR	MAY	JUNE	JULY	AUGUST	SEPT	OCT	NOV	DEC
Total income												
Expenses												
Advert/mktg												
Bad debts												
Bank and cc chgs												
Staff benefits												
Car(s)												
Commissions												
Cost of goods												
Consultants												
Depreciation												
Dues												
Entertainment												
Freight												
Insurance												
Interest expense												
Janitorial/cleaning												
Miscellaneous												
Office supplies												
Pensions												
Rent												
Repairs												
Refunds/returns												
Services												
Taxes												
Telephone												
TOTAL EXPENSE												

From *The Coaching Starter Kit* by CoachVille.com, published by W.W. Norton & Company, Inc.

Business Plan: 5-Year Projection

INCOME	200_	200_	200_	200_	200_	200_	TOTAL
Total income							
Expenses							
Advert/mktg							
Bad debts							
Bank and cc chgs							
Staff benefits							
Car(s)							
Commissions							
Cost of goods							
Consultants							
Depreciation							
Dues							
Entertainment							
Freight							
Insurance							
Interest expense							
Janitorial/cleaning							
Miscellaneous							
Office supplies							
Pensions							
Rent							
Repairs							
Refunds/returns							
Services							
Taxes							
Telephone							
TOTAL EXPENSE							
WHAT'S LEFT							
USES FOR IT							

From *The Coaching Starter Kit* by CoachVille.com, published by W.W. Norton & Company, Inc.

177

Business Budget

MONTHS	1	2	3	4	5	6
SALES						
COST OF SALES						
GROSS PROFIT						
VARIABLE EXPENSES						
Salaries						
Payroll taxes						
Advertising						
Automobile						
Dues and subscriptions						
Legal and accounting						
Supplies						
Telephone						
Utilities						
Miscellaneous						
TOTAL VARIABLE EXPENSES						
FIXED EXPENSES						
Depreciation						
Insurance						
Rent						
Taxes and licenses						
Interest only						
TOTAL FIXED EXPENSES						
TOTAL EXPENSES						
NET PROFIT (LOSS) BEFORE TAXES						
CUMULATIVE PROFIT (LOSS)						

MONTHS	7	8	9	10	11	12
SALES						
COST OF SALES						
GROSS PROFIT						
VARIABLE EXPENSES						
Salaries						
Payroll taxes						
Advertising						
Automobile						
Dues and subscriptions						
Legal and accounting						
Supplies						
Telephone						
Utilities						
Miscellaneous						
TOTAL VARIABLE EXPENSES						
FIXED EXPENSES						
Depreciation						
Insurance						
Rent						
Taxes and licenses						
Interest only						
TOTAL FIXED EXPENSES						
TOTAL EXPENSES						
NET PROFIT (LOSS) BEFORE TAXES						
CUMULATIVE PROFIT (LOSS)						

From The Coaching Starter Kit by CoachVille.com, published by W.W. Norton & Company, Inc.

E-COACHING

98 Steps to Establish, Market, and Manage a Successful Virtual University

A "Virtual University" is a software product and hosting service that provides Internet and teleconferencing services to help build and manage a network of people. It's an ideal tool for coaches to extend their coaching services, and it can be administered directly from your desktop.

Starting a virtual university? Here's your checklist?

I. BEFORE YOU START: PLANNING, PREPARATION, AND TESTING

❏ Set first year goals for number of students, instructors, classes, and revenue.

❏ Arrange for a teleconferencing bridge (a telephone line where up to 150 people can be on the line simultaneously) for teleclasses.

❏ Pick a name for your virtual university and get a matching Internet domain name.

❏ Create your virtual university website or adapt your current website to list it.

❏ Ask around to find out what types of classes people in your network are interested in.

❏ Arrange for a credit card merchant account.

❏ Set up e-mail addresses, phone, and fax numbers for registration.

❏ Set up autoresponders for class brochures and general information.

❏ Obtain a business license and bank account in the virtual university's name.

❏ Set a budget of between $1,000-$25,000 to start.

2. TELECLASS DESIGN ELEMENTS

❏ Pick a class title that includes the focus, the promise, and the benefit.

❏ Identify the learning objectives for each class and class session.

❏ Identify the distinctions, models, or diagrams to share in each session.

❏ Identify the three to five key points you want to make for each class session.

❏ Identify the discussion questions for each class session.

❏ Outline and timeline the content and flow of each class.

❏ Determine what workbooks, checklists, materials, etc. you want your students to have.

❏ Identify the extra support that you can offer for students in your class.

❏ Identify the special benefits to the student.

❏ Write a snappy but personable class description for your website or newsletter.

3. CURRICULUM FORMAT, DESIGN, AND CONTENT

❏ Identify the subjects in which you want to offer classes.

❏ Create the titles for at least ten classes to offer.

❏ Find a way to package, bundle, or link these classes to make it a program.

❏ Write the instructor's profile, credentials, and philosophy on your website and include a photo.

❏ Find and hire qualified teleclass leaders.

❏ Select the best time and day for your classes.

❏ Select optimal class sizes.

❏ Set up a student-only area at your site for each class.

❏ Set a tuition level at which people will easily enroll.

❏ Lead a developmental session of your class ideas as a test.

4. TELECLASS LEADING SKILLS

❏ Know how to grab the students' attention in the first four minutes of the TeleClass.

❏ Learn how to manage the energy, flow, and discussions of 25-150 individuals.

From *The Coaching Starter Kit* by CoachVille.com, published by W.W. Norton & Company, Inc.
Form courtesy of and copyrighted by Thomas Leonard

❑ Know how to generate involvement and discussion among participants.

❑ Discover and develop your strongest—yet warmest—speaking/leading voice.

❑ Know what to do if the unexpected happens in a class.

❑ Learn how to properly acknowledge and endorse what participants say.

❑ Learn how to rephrase and clarify what participants say.

❑ Learn how weave in the comments of participants during the call.

❑ Learn how to emotionally impact the participants.

❑ Fix your communication or style problems and flaws.

5. TELECLASS REGISTRATION, ADMINISTRATION

❑ Write and prepare welcome letters for all classes.

❑ Maintain a class list with full contact information.

❑ E-mail students a reminder twice before the first session date.

❑ Provide a secure way for students to pay online at your website.

❑ Maintain a calendar of classes, times, bridges, and instructors.

❑ Develop an automated, online student registration system like TeleClass.com.

❑ Design, request, collect, and track evaluations for every class and instructor.

❑ Have someone take notes and e-mail them to students right after class (and post on site).

❑ Have the next class ready for students to transition/upgrade into.

❑ Have someone who can offer technical and web support by phone or e-mail.

6. TELECLASS MARKETING

❑ Start a daily or weekly newsletter or tip broadcast to spread the word.

❑ Ask others to share your classes and virtual university with their e-network.

❑ List your virtual university and classes on the major search engines.

❑ Attract media attention.

❑ Offer free classes as a way to build a database and goodwill.

❑ List your TeleClasses on the various TeleClass listing services.

❑ Write/distribute a report/top-ten list related to your class topics/virtual university focus.

❑ Offer an affiliate/associate program like TeleClass.com.

❑ Offer an online self-test to attract people's attention.

❑ Offer early-bird discounts or special bundles. These work.

7. RELATED PRODUCTS/SERVICES

❑ Offer archived versions of your TeleClasses for free or a fee.

❑ Offer a certification of some kind.

❑ Offer an online examination.

❑ Write/offer a printed or e-book related to your virtual university class subjects.

❑ Offer an audiotape version of your classes/programs.

❑ License your classes/intellectual property/program to other companies.

❑ Offer a Train-the-Trainer option (instructs others how to teach the material).

❑ Offer live trainings or presentations based on your TeleClass.

❑ Offer an annual membership with discounts or special bundles.

8. CREATING COMMUNITY

❑ Ask students to be on your research and development team for the virtual university or individual classes.

❑ Give prizes, awards and extras for good ideas, performance, referrals, or support.

❑ Invite students to volunteer for projects or research.

❑ Create a culture that attracts the kind of people you want to be customers.

❑ Offer seemingly unrelated classes that would appeal to your market.

❑ Add special call-in days, web-based resources/links, and fun stuff to your database.

❑ Become the host of a network even larger than your virtual university.

❑ Ask your students to tell you what you should be adding/offering.

❑ Send out a personal, weekly newsletter/update to your members with inside news.

9. ADVANCED FEATURES, BELLS, AND WHISTLES

❑ Have your courses translated into other languages.

❑ Offer a synchronized TeleClass and web page whiteboard or visuals.

❑ Package your TeleClass to be completely web-delivered/computer-based.

❑ Offer an online examination to test student's knowledge/comprehension.

❑ Offer RealVideo classes (archived or live).

❑ Offer courses by daily e-mail—a lesson/step each day in sequential fashion.

❑ Offer an online system for students to give reviews, evaluations, and testimonials of each class/instructor.

❑ Create a web page and/or site for each class, along with meta tags so search engines can find your school/class.

❑ Provide a directory of your students.

❑ Offer discounts for services and products related to your class, program, or school.

10. KEY SUCCESS STRATEGIES

❑ Create a program, not just a bunch of TeleClasses.

❑ Link up with a strategic partner/affiliate who can benefit from the TeleClass format.

❑ Keep experimenting until you find classes that people most want to take. Expand your initial focus if needed.

❑ Give a ton of stuff away as a way to get started and build momentum and your network.

❑ If you're not a great TeleClass leader, become one quickly or hire someone who is.

❑ Keep plugging away for local or national media attention.

❑ Get in the business of creating intellectual property, not just leading TeleClasses.

❑ Offer classes that help people make more money, get ahead/succeed, look better, feel better, or learn a new skill.

❑ Be patient. It takes time (two to three years) to build your network and for people to respond to your class offerings.

❑ Target market segments/industry groups according to where referrals come from..

From *The Coaching Starter Kit* by CoachVille.com, published by W. W. Norton & Company, Inc.
Form courtesy of and copyrighted by Thomas Leonard

TELECLASSES

90+ Skills and Steps to Design and Lead TeleClasses

Whereas e-coaching is coaching done via Internet communication, TeleClass coaching is performed over the telephone.

1. OWN THE TELECLASS

- ❏ Teach only what you enjoy teaching
- ❏ Don't be wimpy or too soft
- ❏ Project your voice to reach people
- ❏ Teach to one person at a time
- ❏ Make individuals feel special
- ❏ Come to the class eager to learn
- ❏ Bond with the strongest three people
- ❏ Challenge students to think big
- ❏ Plant many seeds but don't reap yet
- ❏ Tailor class to students' needs

2. DESIGN THE TELECLASS

- ❏ Why are you leading this TeleClass?
- ❏ How many sessions should it be?
- ❏ How do you want the students to change?
- ❏ What do you want them to learn?
- ❏ What three distinctions are important?
- ❏ What three questions should I ask?
- ❏ What is compelling about this class?
- ❏ What long-term effect do I want for students?
- ❏ What else do I want to offer them?
- ❏ What should they do after the class?

3. PREPARE FOR THE TELECLASS

- ❏ Write up your class outline
- ❏ Ask five smart people for suggestions
- ❏ Set a date for your TeleClass
- ❏ Arrange for a telebridge
- ❏ Write up a class description/title
- ❏ Announce/promote/fill TeleClass
- ❏ Invite five key, well-connected people
- ❏ Spend ten minutes with each registrant, finding out what they most want out of the class
- ❏ Run a test class first
- ❏ Write up class notes and share

4. BASIC LEADING SKILLS

- ❏ Weave in earlier student comments
- ❏ Strongly endorse what students say
- ❏ Ask students for clarification
- ❏ Ask students for more information
- ❏ Provide interesting facts
- ❏ Focus on strongest students
- ❏ Include/call on quiet students
- ❏ Ask big, provoking questions
- ❏ Make people feel smart/special
- ❏ Debrief at the end of the call

5. INTERMEDIATE SKILLS

- ❏ Use coaching models/diagrams
- ❏ Believe in the student's intelligence
- ❏ Provoke reactions to foster discussion
- ❏ Challenge students to be honest
- ❏ Solve problems for students
- ❏ Help students to network with each other outside of class
- ❏ Offer extras for students after class
- ❏ Go with the flow/needs of the students

From *The Coaching Starter Kit* by CoachVille.com, published by W. W. Norton & Company, Inc.

185

❑ Create wisdom from student's shares

❑ Create credibility by asking for topic-based testimonials

6. ADVANCED SKILLS

❑ Frame the call at the beginning

❑ Identify/build up the class's stars

❑ Tell a humanizing story about yourself

❑ Point to a developmental path

❑ Articulate what is occurring

❑ Identify a shift one might make

❑ Get students to laugh at themselves, life, you, their goals, their problems, and each other

❑ Help students to share themselves

❑ Tell them how they might misinterpret

7. MAKING YOUR POINT

❑ Use metaphors/similes/analogies

❑ Paint a picture/visual image

❑ Package points into messages

❑ Rephrase what a student says

❑ Demonstrate (roleplay) a point/skill

❑ Create context/relevance

❑ Reveal benefits of your point

❑ Draw distinctions/progressions

❑ Plant seeds that will sprout later

❑ Create a gap/play 'what if?'

8. HANDLING DIFFICULT STUDENTS

❑ Interrupt the space pig

❑ Bring out the mouse

❑ Quiet down the boomer

❑ Notch down the impresser

❑ Explain for the clarifier

❑ Cut off the resident coach

❑ Refocus the naysayer

❑ Challenge the cliché user

❑ Evolve the linear

9. MISTAKES TO AVOID

❑ Don't lecture continuously

❑ Don't assume you communicate well

❑ Don't assume class will fill by itself

❑ Don't lose control of the class

❑ Don't worry if students don't like you

❑ Don't stop learning from students

❑ Don't teach what you don't believe in

❑ Don't teach alone

❑ Don't get your emotional needs met by leading TeleClasses

10. COMMUNICATION SKILLS

❑ Tone is warm enough to charm across 3,000 miles

❑ Pace is fast enough to keep people's attention

❑ Volume is loud enough to reach people

❑ Pitch is deep enough

❑ Vocabulary is extensive enough to expand upon what students are saying

❑ Hearing is sharp enough to pick up subtleties

❑ Students feel heard versus reacted to

❑ Delivery is strong and confident

❑ Transition/segue from one point to another is smooth

❑ Leader is positive in everything he/she says

Part 3

Marketing Your Practice

Chapter 7

Marketing Essentials

PR AND PRESS KITS
Media Sound Bites

KEY POINTS TO MAKE ABOUT COACHING

1. Coaching is distinct from consulting, therapy, and friendship. All coaches are consultants; few consultants are coaches.

2. The coach/client relationship is a designed alliance focusing on maximizing opportunities, not just on solving problems.

3. People hire a coach because they want more of something (money, time, happiness, success, freedom) or less of something (frustration, tolerations, delays).

4. A coach is trained to work with a client on both personal and business goals. A therapist works on issues. There's a big difference.

5. Coaching works because of the synergy resulting from a professional partnership.

6. Few people need a coach; most people want a coach.

7. Coaches are experts in people and success, not just problem-solving.

8. Coaching has become a very popular profession lately, offering geographic flexibility, fulfilling work with a healthy clientele, low emotional costs (very little travel, stress, commuting, or workplace problems), and the reward of continuing personal and professional development.

9. There are coaches in virtually every state in the U.S. and in at least thirty countries.

10. It has become common to have a coach. The question will be "Who is your coach?" not "Do you have a coach?"

11. One source of the demand for coaches and coaching comes from the increasing number of entrepreneurs and infopreneurs seeking to be successful in an extremely competitive marketplace. The right coach gives a professional or business owner a competitive advantage.

12. The newest area of growth in the coaching industry will be international during the next decade. With a coach, anyone in the world can access this style of creative-thinking and support. And as more coaches set up shop in their own countries, the coaching style will reflect the local culture.

13. Thanks to the web and the Internet, the best advice in the world can be accessed and shared from anywhere.

14. When a client hires a coach in Minneapolis, for example, they are also getting access to an international network of coaches and experts; access to solutions and answers are usually just a phone call—or mouse click—away.

15. As Americans put up with less and expect more out of life, they'll find a willing and supportive partner in a professional coach.

16. Having it all is just the beginning. Most Americans today want it all without having to pay the price. With coaching, this becomes possible. You may not get it all, but you can get all that matters most.

17. Coaching is becoming popular as time becomes more valuable. Today, few of us can afford the steep learning curve of life. What would it be like to be wise, happy, and successful this year versus waiting a decade or two?

From *The Coaching Starter Kit* by CoachVille.com, published by W. W. Norton & Company, Inc.
Form courtesy of and copyrighted by Thomas Leonard

18. The compelling reason people have for hiring a coach: they are just unwilling to wait to get what they want. They now turn to an outside expert to help them get what they most want, in a healthier, more productive, and sustainable way.

19. Self-help is a distant second to coaching. Who has the patience to work alone? That's the old way.

20. The best Olympic skaters all have a coach that they've bonded with, who brings out their best. Doesn't everyone deserve to have a coach who brings out their best?

21. You don't buy a coaching service, you hire a coach and build a relationship.

22. There are approximately 10,000 full-time coaches in the U.S. earning between $30,000 and $150,000 per year.

23. Eighty percent of coaches work primarily over the phone versus in person, and have a national practice.

24. The profession is in its infancy. Coaching is a new profession, started in the last ten years and formalized in the past six years.

25. The profession is developing its credibility and stature based on the success of coaches' clients, not just the success of coaches.

26. Clients usually pay a monthly fee ranging from $200-$500 to their coach for four weekly sessions. There are no other charges/fees. It's rare that a coach contracts for a percentage or contingency-type fee or reward.

27. Some senior coaches charge an entrepreneur or corporate client an annual retainer or program fee of $5,000-$250,000.

28. Ninety-five percent of coaches do not require an ongoing contract; clients are free to leave if desired.

29. A client works with the same coach for an average of one year (and this term is increasing).

30. Most coaches coach an average of thirty-eight clients each week, after being in the field for two years.

31. The average age of coaches is forty-seven years old. The range is from thirty to seventy.

32. Forty-three percent of coaches are men; 57 percent are women.

33. Ninety percent of coaches have at least an undergraduate degree; 52 percent have a graduate degree; 7 percent hold a doctorate.

34. Backgrounds of coaches reported (from most to least): consultants, mental health professionals, management, T&D/HR, financial consultants and CPAs, theater and professional speakers, engineers, sales.

35. Client types being coached (most to least, all coaches reported a combination):

Professionals = 86%

Entrepreneurs = 60%

Leaders = 45%

Creative = 42%

CEOs/Execs = 38%

Transitioning = 37%

From *The Coaching Starter Kit* by CoachVille.com, published by W. W. Norton & Company, Inc. Form courtesy of and copyrighted by Thomas Leonard

COACHING STORY ANGLES

COACHING IS A LUCRATIVE, EMERGING PROFESSION

If the pressures of modern life are creating a demand for coaches, the appeal of the coach's working lifestyle is also creating a growing supply. Some benefits to the coach include: geographic flexibility; high hourly rate ($100-$200); work mostly by phone (or e-mail, if you choose); paid monthly in advance; rewarding clients; low entry costs to the field; a chance to help others; great community of coaches with whom to become colleagues/friends; and a chance to grow.

COACHING CAN BRING ABOUT DRAMATIC RESULTS

Coaches can help clients achieve dramatic results. Some real-life examples: executing the successful turnaround of Macy's (and saving the parade!); convincing the resistant Pentagon to create a memorial in Arlington National Cemetery for the victims of Pan Am flight 103; transforming a heroin-addicted convict to a summa cum laude, double master's-degreed professional; surviving cancer; making peace with an estranged parent the night before he or she dies; and moving from $100K to $800K in revenues in nine months. Ask for interviews with such coaches and clients.

BABY BOOMERS TAKE TO COACHING

Coach U recently polled the coaching community to find out what the presence of baby boomers (35- to 50-year-olds) was. We found that of the 2,000 coaches in the U.S., 1,600, or four out of five, are baby boomers. Each coach has an average of 13 boomer-aged clients, as well. There are some 26,000 boomers that are clients of coaches today. And it's growing rapidly.

COACHING AS THE NEXT GENERATION OF THERAPY

Therapists want healthier clients; healthier clients want more than therapy offers, and enjoy coaching more. Twenty percent of coaches' clients are also in therapy. Therapists like coaching because it's more fun and intellectually challenging, and there's no insurance to worry about, and it can be done on the phone. As coach Laura Berman-Fortgang, says, "I specialize in growth, not rescue." Ask for interviews with psychologists who have happily left counseling for coaching.

CYBERCOACHING: A HOT NEW NICHE!

Coaches who coach their clients via e-mail are called cybercoaches. It's a special niche that requires good online and writing skills.

COACHING IS THE PERFECT RETIREMENT PROFESSION

Why would you want to be a coach when you retire from another career? Because clients appreciate your wisdom; compensation is excellent at $100-200 an hour; it's a flexible job you can have for the rest of your life; you're not disconnected from a strong professional community like many other retirees; coaching is intellectually, emotionally, and spiritually stimulating; it keeps you young; you're making a significant and positive contribution to society; you have a focus and purpose for your day; you don't have to use a computer or even drive a car if you don't want to—most coaches do their client sessions on the telephone; and there are already many people well over the age of 50 who have succeeded at this profession and love their lives now more than ever. Ask for contact numbers of successful coaches in their golden years.

AN INCREDIBLE VARIETY OF COACHING NICHES

The best coaches seem to specialize in something about which they know a lot. There are parent coaches, career coaches, chemotherapy coaches, cop coaches, rock-'n-roll band coaches, attraction coaches, book marketing coaches, wellness coaches, chronic-care coaches, money coaches, Generation X coaches, web coaches, stockbroker coaches, healthcare professional coaches, and attorney coaches. Ask for interviews with coaches in the niche you're interested in.

HOW COACHING EMERGED FROM THE DOWNSIZING TREND

Two ways: People who have been laid off and can't find work elsewhere due to their age are becoming self-employed coaches. Corporations who are having to lay off people are turning to coaches for outplacement assistance.

COACHES SHOW CLIENTS HOW TO SIMPLIFY THEIR LIVES

Downshifting, living simply, voluntary simplicity—whatever you want to call it, a high percentage of coaches have done this successfully with their own lives and are coaching clients to do so as well.

The Media Pitch

1. **Write a personal letter to the media outlet you want to contact.**

   Address your letter to the appropriate editor or producer by calling first and asking. Spell their name correctly. Spell everything correctly.

2. **Use your professionally-printed letterhead.**

3. **Whet their appetite.**

   Give them a story idea that they can't get out of their mind. Raise questions to which they must find out the answer.

4. **What's the story hook?**

   Capture their attention in the first paragraph with what's most compelling, time-sensitive, local, newsworthy, and beguiling about your topic. If they are available, use good statistics to back up your claims, or quote credentialed experts. Tell them why they need to do this story immediately. (You don't want your letter to get filed in their "Future Story Ideas" file— it's a black hole.)

5. **Give several brief but interesting examples, testimonials, or success stories to illustrate your point.**

   (Three ways you've coached clients out of bankruptcy, for example.)

6. **Demonstrate extreme familiarity with the media outlet.**

   You know what they would and wouldn't publish and it shows in your letter.

7. **Help them envision the article or segment by describing how it might be executed.**

   Give several different angles (e.g., a "round-up" article of coaches in different niches, or how you coached a diabetic client to make a dramatic change in their life, to be published during National Diabetes Awareness Month)

8. **Tell them why you are the perfect interview for this article.**

   But don't say, "I'm the perfect interview for this because . . ." Demonstrate it through a concise description of your credentials that relates to the story idea you're proposing. Don't tell them everything you do/have done because it dilutes the power of the pitch. Stay focused. (For example, if you're pitching a story on coaching rock bands, they probably don't need to know you're an R.N. in the pitch letter.)

9. **Limit your letter to one or two pages maximum.**

10. **Make it easy for them to contact you.**

11. **Include a press kit if you have one and can afford it.**

    Otherwise, enclose copies of important related articles that have already been published. Let them know about the coaching organizations you belong to and how to contact the PR person there for more information.

12. **Spell-check and proofread.**

    Then have someone else proofread your letter before it is mailed.

13. **Follow up by phone two to three days after the letter has arrived to see if there is any interest.**

    Don't be a pest by alerting the media every time you get a new client. Instead, create a regular mailing list of reporters with whom you're interested in developing relationships and send them a brief update letter approximately once a quarter. Follow the above advice in every correspondence with them.

From *The Coaching Starter Kit* by CoachVille.com, published by W. W. Norton & Company, Inc.
Form courtesy of and copyrighted by Amy Watson, The Publicity Coach

195

Speaking with Reporters

When a reporter contacts you about a story they're working on, or you receive a publicity lead, make sure you put your best foot forward in responding to them:

1. Before responding, be clear on their topic, questions, and the type of expertise they seek. Only respond if you fit the bill.

2. Don't dilute the power of your response by adding extraneous information—stick to the topic.

3. Be concise and use compelling language.

4. Tell them something they don't expect to hear, but make sure you can back up your opinion with facts and anecdotes.

5. Teach them something new about their subject—be a resource.

6. Be brief, but give them juicy morsels of information. At this stage, this is not yet an interview—you're just trying to whet their appetite so they ask for one.

7. Provide your credentials in short form. For example, "I am a full-time business plan writing coach with twenty years of experience as an entrepreneur and consultant. I have worked with teams at Microsoft, 3M, and Paine Webber. I directed the writing of the turnaround business plan for Taco Bell." Only include elements germane to the reporter's topic—don't try to be all things to all people. Focus your authority in their area of interest and you'll be the most appealing expert for them to interview.

8. Include all your contact information: name, title, company, address, phone numbers (with time zone and best times to call), fax, and e-mail address. If you have a good professional website, include the URL.

9. Spell-check, grammar-check, and proofread! Be punctual in your response—get back to them within twelve hours or well within their deadline.

From *The Coaching Starter Kit* by CoachVille.com, published by W. W. Norton & Company, Inc.
Form courtesy of and copyrighted by Amy Watson, The Publicity Coach

Your Press Kit

If you receive a publicity lead or are contacted by an interested reporter, it is a good idea to have a press kit prepared for them.

- Folder (9 x12) with pocket (8.5 x 11 paper will fit inside) with logo on outside
- Envelope (10 x 13) to mail it in
- Business card to put in diagonal cuts in pocket
- Press release(s)
- Bio
- Picture printed on card stock with logo and phone number in margin
- Published articles that you've written
- Unpublished articles you've written the media can use
- Published articles written about you
- Published articles supporting your cause or industry
- Brochures, fliers, and other marketing materials
- Fact sheets on company background, key points, topics on which you're an expert, top ten lists, etc.
- Testimonials and success stories
- Samples of your work (guides, workbooks, checklists, etc.)
- Cover letter or legible, personal, hand-written notes

MAKE THE NEWS: PRACTICAL PUBLICITY STUNTS THAT WORK

1. Conduct a survey or opinion poll
2. Report a finding
3. Release a study
4. Dig up statistics
5. Get some endorsements that lend credibility
6. Self-publish a small, free guide, magazine, or newsletter
7. Gather success stories from your customers and tell a tale
8. Share off-beat, informative, and cutting-edge ideas
9. Offer opinions about growing trends
10. Make predictions
11. Do something interesting and meaningful that benefits someone besides yourself
12. Become an expert in something
13. Write a book
14. Offer a grant to a deserving someone in need
15. Report a significant business-related development within your organization
16. Package your organization's news in the context of a national trend
17. Share an advance in understanding
18. Point to a sign of the times

From *The Coaching Starter Kit* by CoachVille.com, published by W.W. Norton & Company, Inc.

199

More PR Tips

DO-IT-YOURSELF PR: 8 WAYS TO GET YOUR PUBLICITY MACHINE GOING

1. Establish a good contact database.

2. Start collecting media contacts with whom you want to build relationships.

3. Send a letter of introduction, following the 13 components of a successful media pitch (see The Media Pitch). Send a press kit if you can afford it.

4. What goes into a press kit: folder stuffed with press releases, your bio, your picture, articles you've written or that have been written about you or your clients' success, testimonials/success stories, brochures, marketing materials, miscellaneous items, your business card.

5. Stay in the forefront of the journalist's mind by staying in touch. Every two to three months, send them short, useful things you've written that they can publish or read on-air.

6. Send letters instead of press releases to add a personal touch.

7. Get a professional photo taken for use by the media.

8. Leverage your media coverage. When a story comes out, buy reprints to use in your press kit or marketing materials. Hand them out at presentations, send to clients and prospects.

10 STEPS TO GETTING YOUR COACHING ARTICLE PUBLISHED

One way to see your name in print is to offer to author an article for a publication. This is a wonderful marketing tool that helps establish your credentials as an expert and gives you far more editorial freedom than an article about you written by someone else. Here's how to get started:

1. Make or buy a list of your target publications. Choose those that would be the most interested in your particular coaching niche (e.g., *Wine Business Monthly* if you coach enologists), or those whose audiences you have something in common with (*Coastal Living* if you moved to Malibu to coach).

2. Prioritize these publications. Which do you want to appear in first? Look at your marketing plan to help you decide.

3. Call and find out if the publications have "writer's guidelines" you can request. If so, they often ask that you do so in writing and include a self-addressed stamped envelope. Be sure to include this in every piece of correspondence to a publication when you are proposing to be the author of the article.

4. The writer's guidelines should indicate if the publication does indeed accept submissions from non-staff writers like you. If so, read six to twelve months worth of back issues to familiarize yourself with all the publication's nuances. Find the column or section that repeatedly uses the type of article you're planning on submitting, and study the style, voice, and format.

5. Sometimes writer's guidelines are unclear or too brief to be helpful. If this is the case, call the publication and ask to speak to the managing editor. Ask them to clarify how they like to be approached for an article submission by an expert (as opposed to a freelance journalist). Have several story angles prepared to pitch to them. Find out if they want a "query letter," which is a one- to two-page proposal of the article you have in mind, or if they prefer to see the completed manuscript first. Find out to whom you should address the pitch and how to spell their name.

6. Send your query or manuscript only after having a super-literate friend or writing consultant scrutinize it.

7. Enclose your resumé or your marketing materials with copies of any other high-quality published work of yours, articles about you or others that pertain to coaching and are relevant to sell the editor on your idea.

8. If you send the full manuscript, don't forget to include a cover letter telling the editor briefly what you are sending them, and for what section or column it is meant. Include a brief background about yourself and the relevance of your piece to the editor's audience.

9. Don't forget your self-addressed stamped envelope with the proper amount of postage!

10. If the publication is not interested in your article, you'll probably only get back a pre-printed form letter indicating so. Otherwise, the editor will most likely call you with the good news!

HOW TO LEVERAGE MEDIA COVERAGE

- Announce to everyone you know that the publicity is coming out, and when and where

- Make tapes/clips of it and send it to other media and prospective clients

- Put reprints of articles in your press kit

- Be prepared for a lot of new business so you're investment in publicity won't be wasted

- Use reprints of articles as powerful marketing tools:

    1. As an insert in your company's media kit

    2. As a third-party endorsement incorporated into your sales presentation

    3. As a handout at trade shows, conventions, and conferences

    4. As a direct mail piece to help increase market share

    5. As a tool for informing and inspiring your team

INTERNET

97 Ways to Market Yourself and Your Site on the Internet

Below is a list of ten primary marketing strategies. I've compiled one hundred specific things you can do to become more successful on the Internet.

1. BE FINDABLE ON SEARCH ENGINES & DIRECTORIES

❑ I have inserted meta tags on my home page.

❑ I have used the right words in the meta tags to attract the right visitors.

❑ I have put meta tags on every page of my website.

❑ I have used a descriptive title for each of my pages.

❑ I have listed my site on the top ten search engines (yahoo, google, lycos, etc.).

❑ I have tested how well my site ranks on the search engines.

❑ I have listed my site on at least five directories related to my field/interests.

❑ I have learned how search engines work and have adjusted my meta tags/format to attract more visitors.

❑ I have listed myself on at least twenty-five relevant directories.

___ **Section Score**

2. ARRANGE FOR CROSSLINKS AND INCREASE YOUR EXPOSURE

❑ I know how many links to my site there are.

❑ There is a link from at least ten other sites to my site.

❑ I have a favorite links page with at least twenty listings.

❑ I am part of a web ring or am hosting a web ring.

❑ I have applied to get my site linked from the award-granting sites.

❑ I post to newsgroups.

❑ I join/get on ICQ.

❑ I offer a membership and give people a reason to link to my sites from theirs.

❑ I have contacted fifty colleagues to link to my site (and mine to theirs).

❑ I have listed my site on professional associations' directories.

❑ I have approached writers/editors of twenty e-zines and asked them to put me on their contact list.

___ **Section Score**

3. PROVIDE VALUABLE CONTENT AT YOUR SITE

❑ I have at least ten top 10 lists that share knowledge I have about my subject/expertise.

❑ I have identified the top four types of people who will visit my site.

❑ I offer a track for each of them to follow, or solutions to their concerns, at my site.

❑ I have written and posted an e-book at my site that visitors can download for free or purchase.

❑ I have included RealAudio files at my site containing valuable information.

❑ I have created a self-test that visitors can take and score themselves.

❑ I offer a FAQs/Q&A section to answer questions about my product/service.

❑ My site is a portal containing many links to other sites related to my profession or industry.

❑ I have included a searchable index of my e-tips.

From *The Coaching Starter Kit* by CoachVille.com, published by W. W. Norton & Company, Inc.
Form courtesy of and copyrighted by Thomas Leonard

❑ I offer situational advice to anyone visiting.

___ **Section Score**

4. OFFER A FREE E-NEWSLETTER OR E-TIP BROADCAST

❑ I have selected a topic for my e-news or e-tip.

❑ I have chosen the format and frequency of my broadcast.

❑ I have written three issues and sent them out to at least one hundred people who I know.

❑ I have listed my e-newsletter with five repositories.

❑ I have automated the sub/unsubscribe process.

❑ I encourage subscribers to pass along the e-news/tip broadcast to anyone they wish.

❑ Subscribing/unsubscribing instructions are at the top/bottom of each broadcast.

❑ I ask my subscribers for feedback, comments, and questions and I respond to these.

❑ I offer free giveaways or sales as a plug at the bottom of each broadcast.

___ **Section Score**

5. HAVE A WELL-DESIGNED WEBSITE

❑ My site gives visitors immediate access/answers to 90 percent of visitors.

❑ My site looks professional.

❑ The graphics are high quality.

❑ I prompt visitors to subscribe to my newsletter.

❑ I offer a bulletin board/discussion list where visitors can post comments/questions.

❑ I've designed my site to lead people through it, step by step.

❑ I've designed my site to lead people, step by step, to buy something at my site.

❑ I have a photograph of myself on my site.

___ **Section Score**

6. WORK WITH THE MEDIA

❑ I've written a press release announcing my site, product, or service.

❑ I've broadcast/distributed this press release.

❑ I am giving something away for free and have let the media know about this.

❑ I have let everyone in my network know that I am available for media interviews on a particular subject.

❑ I've written a book and had it published.

❑ I have been mentioned or featured in someone else's book.

❑ I've contacted 500 radio stations that do interviews and offered myself as a guest.

❑ I've written a pitch letter to the local news media suggesting a story that relates to my work/site.

❑ I've conducted a poll and released the results of the poll to the media.

❑ I've sent a video of myself to the morning TV talk shows and suggested a topic.

___ **Section Score**

7. ADVERTISE AND PROMOTE

❑ I've arranged for owners of lists to let me market my site/services/products via their e-newsletter/tips.

From *The Coaching Starter Kit* by CoachVille.com, published by W. W. Norton & Company, Inc. Form courtesy of and copyrighted by Thomas Leonard

❑ I've purchased at least 10,000 exposures for my Internet banner advertisements.

❑ I advertise in opt-in mailing lists

❑ I've purchased promotional items with my web address.

❑ I've put my web and e-mail address on my business cards and letterhead.

❑ I've sponsored a website.

❑ I've had at least one banner ad created.

❑ I use a complete signature on my e-mail announcing all that I offer.

❑ I have purchased an opt-in mailing list.

❑ I have run classified ads selling my product or service.

____ **Section Score**

8. BECOME THE HOST OF A NETWORK

❑ Offer a tip broadcast/e-newsletter.

❑ Offer a directory/portal.

❑ Offer fee/free TeleClasses.

❑ Invite visitors to local meetings.

❑ Host a discussion group.

❑ Offer a certification program.

❑ Become a formal information association.

❑ Launch a virtual university.

❑ Run a contest.

❑ Offer free support/advice.

____ **Section Score**

9. OFFER LOTS OF GIVEAWAYS AND GOODS FOR SALE

❑ Products

❑ Services

❑ Programs

❑ Classes

❑ Reports/Information

❑ Books/Tapes

❑ Memberships

❑ E-books

❑ Agents/affiliate programs

❑ Advice and consulting

____ **Section Score**

10. KEEP EXPERIMENTING

❑ Create a website that reflects/expresses what is most important to you.

❑ Keep experimenting to see what draws people in.

❑ Add more websites, just for the fun of it.

❑ Offer links from your site to new resources that your visitors may want to know about.

❑ Sponsor a brainstorming session once a month with your colleagues/friends.

❑ Keep testing the ranking of your site on the search engines (and keep tweaking).

❑ Spend an hour a month surfing other related sites and adapting some of their ideas to improve your own site.

❑ Identify a need that the public has and create a website to serve that need even if unrelated to your current knowledge or service.

❑ Take a TeleClass or buy a book on Internet marketing to see what's new.

❑ Add RealVideo to your site for a stronger punch and more traffic.

____ **Section Score**

From *The Coaching Starter Kit* by CoachVille.com, published by W. W. Norton & Company, Inc.
Form courtesy of and copyrighted by Thomas Leonard

205

Website Design and Function

ELEMENTS OF A TERRIFIC WEBSITE

This checklist has been designed for service professionals, but it is also useful for anyone setting up a website and/or perfecting their website.

1. DESIGN, RESEARCH, AND PLANNING

❏ I've selected a great .com domain name and have reserved it.

❏ I have described/outlined the four things that the people coming to my website will likely be looking for/wanting.

❏ I've downloaded/purchased an HTML software program that I like.

❏ I understand at least the very basics of raw HTML.

❏ I have sketched out at least ten of the pages of my site and how they link together.

❏ I have found at least ten well-designed sites of competitors and have made a list of the twenty-five design elements I want on my site.

❏ I've have selected a web host provider.

❏ I've got someone I can call or e-mail when I get stuck on my web page.

❏ I've obtained a domain name in my name if available.

❏ I know my financial and time budget for this website.

___ **Section Score**

2. BASIC WEB DESIGN / HTML SKILLS

❏ I know how to "view source" to see the raw HTML code from any web page.

❏ I know how to set the background color of the web page.

❏ I know how to choose the default font so my web pages look clean.

❏ I know how to insert a graphic into a web page.

❏ I've experimented with at least two online create-a-site systems.

❏ I know how to open a graphics file, add text, and save it as a jpg or gif file.

❏ I know how to transfer files (called FTP) from my website to my Internet provider's computer.

❏ I know to how link pages together.

❏ I know how to create tables and perform basic layout.

___ **Section Score**

3. INCLUDE IMPORTANT DETAILS AND INFORMATION

❏ I use a graphically-appealing company logo/name.

❏ My toll-free, toll phone, and fax numbers are on each page.

❏ A copyright notice is on each page.

❏ The title appears on each HTML page.

❏ I provide the city and/or state where I am located (address optional—don't provide it if a residence, for security reasons).

❏ The "last updated" date is included on the home page and selected pages.

❏ I've included a professional photo of myself on my site.

❏ I have included a FAQ (frequently asked questions) section.

❏ Each page has a consistent look and feel.

❏ I have meta tags on each page, not just the home page.

___ **Section Score**

4. BASIC CONTENT

❏ I explain who I am and what makes me special.

From *The Coaching Starter Kit* by CoachVille.com, published by W. W. Norton & Company, Inc.
Form courtesy of and copyrighted by Thomas Leonard

❏ I explain the services I offer and how they work.

❏ I am clear on how much my services/products cost and what one receives for this price.

❏ I have a list of solutions that will appeal to most of my visitors.

❏ I describe at least three benefits to people who use my service/product.

❏ I offer several goods/services for free at my site to get people started.

❏ I have a page containing links that might interest the visitor.

❏ The site is organized around what's important to the visitor, not just what's important to me.

❏ I explain who visits my site and what I can do for them.

❏ I've had someone read my site and help me remove all jargon.

___ **Section Score**

5. TECHNICAL DETAILS

❏ The site is viewable on a 14" monitor with no scrolling needed.

❏ I've viewed my site via other browsers to make sure it looks right.

❏ I've made sure all of my links work.

❏ I have had my HTML validated.

❏ I have verified my meta tags.

❏ Whenever an e-mail address is included, it is hotlinked.

❏ My average page is less than 30K text and 50K graphics.

❏ My e-mail address uses the same domain name as my website domain name.

❏ I've compressed my graphics for fast downloading.

❏ I am getting a traffic report from my web hosting company.

___ **Section Score**

6. GRAPHIC DESIGN AND APPEAL

❏ My site has a professional look.

❏ My art (logos, illustrations) is clean and crisp.

❏ My site looks distinct; it's not a replica of others' in my field.

❏ I use only one or two different fonts per page.

❏ I use interlaced image files (they appear more quickly).

❏ I use only colors that all browsers can display properly.

❏ I chose colors carefully and artfully, not jarringly.

❏ There is a theme to my site; it is an expression of me or of my company.

❏ The names I use for the links make sense even to the fist-time visitor.

___ **Section Score**

7. EASE OF NAVIGATION / INTUITIVE FEEL

❏ The average user is never more than three clicks away from what they'll need.

❏ I don't give the user more than six options on any one page.

❏ I offer a site index.

❏ I use image maps for a clean, easy look.

❏ The visitor is guided as to what to do, see, or go to next.

❏ There are forward, back, top-of-page, and home page buttons throughout the site.

❑ There is a site search engine that is easy to find and that works well.

❑ The visitor doesn't get stuck going down any blind alleys.

❑ I've asked five people to visit my site and tell me what they didn't like about it or found wasn't clear and easy.

❑ I have walked through my site and it flows.

___ **Section Score**

8. SELLING POWER AND EASE OF BUYING

❑ I give the buyer four ways to buy (e-mail, web, phone, fax).

❑ I have packaged my services to make them intriguing and appealing.

❑ I make ordering online a simple, immediate process.

❑ I am using a secure server; clients can sign up online.

❑ Credit card transactions are processed in Real Time.

❑ I include testimonials of others who have used my services.

❑ I offer a guarantee of satisfaction.

❑ I offer enough content to show I know what I'm talking about.

❑ I've established my credibility completely.

❑ There is a mechanism, test, or questions for the visitor to be able to qualify/disqualify themselves as a potential client.

___ **Section Score**

9. MARKETING AND LINKS

❑ I have included properly used meta tags on all of my pages.

❑ Visitors can recommend this site to a friend, right at the site.

❑ I am listed at yahoo and the other search engines.

❑ I offer a free e-newsletter for which people can sign up on the website.

❑ I am linked to at least ten others in my field/industry and they are linked to me.

❑ I know where my site appears on the search engines.

❑ I am part of a web ring.

❑ I mention/refer people to my website in my e-mail signature.

❑ I include my website URL on my stationary, brochures, and marketing tools.

❑ I am part of a professional/trade association that has a listing for me or links to my site.

___ **Section Score**

10. WAYS TO ENGAGE THE VISITOR

❑ I offer a free TeleClass they can sign up for online.

❑ I offer a free newsletter/tip broadcast they can subscribe to online.

❑ I offer a free consultation/sample.

❑ I offer a chat-room at my site.

❑ I offer a discussion board at my site.

❑ I offer a free report (related to my subject/field) via auto-responder.

❑ I offer a book or tape they can buy or get for free.

❑ I offer to refer the visitor to someone who can help them.

❑ I offer the visitor a list of links that will continue their journey.

❑ I offer the visitor a chance to meet me personally.

___ **Section Score**

From *The Coaching Starter Kit* by CoachVille.com, published by W. W. Norton & Company, Inc.
Form courtesy of and copyrighted by Thomas Leonard

Top 5 Things Your Coaching Website Should Be Set up to Do

Gone are the days of the "billboard website" (name, list of services, testimonials, "what is coaching?," etc.). Welcome to the website that actually serves the visitor versus just informing them. Here are the five things that your website should be set up to do when someone visits it.

1. **Capture the visitor's e-mail address**

   Offer whatever you have to in order to get the visitor to type in their e-mail address. Try a free report, e-book, subscription, coaching session, access to information on your website, TeleClass, etc. You need an e-mail address in order to effectively market your visitors. Ease them in closer and closer to your inner circle.

2. **Permit visitors to sign up for free or fee sessions or TeleClasses online—automatically and immediately**

   It is good to give out your telephone number on your site and invite visitors to call you. It's even better if you set up a little calendar with the times and dates you are available so the visitor books themselves into your schedule, right then, when they are at your site.

3. **Demonstrate your expertise and knowledge**

   The stuff that you know and take for granted is like gold to someone who doesn't know it. Why not compile an e-book of your success tips or ten top 10s on your favorite subjects. Or, tape yourself and post as a RealAudio interview so the visitor can hear your voice, which is important given most coaching is done over the telephone.

4. **Help the visitor to buy something you are offering, online**

   Eventually, every coach will have a merchant account and a shopping cart that enables visitors to hire you on the spot, and prepay for your coaching services, e-book, TeleClasses, etc. It's just a matter of time. And once you get started, you'll be hooked!

5. **Directly answer the top five or ten questions that you anticipate your ideal client asking**

   Everyone coming to your site (or any other coaching site) has questions. If you can answer these questions up front, you will be building a relationship with your visitors. Relationships and credibility lead to clients. Ask yourself, "If I was my ideal client, what are the ten questions I would most want straight answers to?" Then, post these prominently on your home page.

From *The Coaching Starter Kit* by CoachVille.com, published by W. W. Norton & Company, Inc.
Form courtesy of and copyrighted by Thomas Leonard

e-Tip Broadcasting

100 STEPS TO SETTING UP A SUCCESSFUL E-NEWS / E-TIP BROADCAST

Want to broadcast an e-newsletter or daily tip? The following checklist should help.

1. BEFORE YOU START: DECISION-MAKING, PLANNING, AND PREPARATION

❑ Set first-year goals: How many subscribers do you want within twelve months?

❑ Select the topic or theme for your broadcast that you will really enjoy writing about.

❑ Figure out why you want to do this and what the benefits are to you.

❑ Identify the ten elements you like about other tips/newsletters that you receive.

❑ Schedule time to write your e-newsletter or tips each week.

❑ Start writing (your first newsletter issue or five tips).

❑ Share your initial writings with ten people and ask for improvements.

❑ Make sure your e-mail program can handle 200 e-mail addresses for broadcasting.

❑ Set up a website or web area to which you can upload your writings/tips.

❑ Decide the level of automation you want your broadcasting system to have.

2. E-NEWSLETTER / TIP DESIGN ELEMENTS— GROUP 1

❑ Title (of tip or newsletter).

❑ Personal news.

❑ Topical news.

❑ Share feedback from readers with everyone.

❑ Provide a situational solution or strategy.

❑ Suggest a change in thinking or behavior.

❑ Pose an interesting question.

❑ Provide a statistic.

❑ Recommend a URL/website link.

❑ Share your opinion.

3. E-NEWSLETTER / TIP DESIGN ELEMENTS— GROUP 2

❑ Quote an expert or authority.

❑ Include a powerful, appropriate quote.

❑ Profile/review a book.

❑ Share a client's story/case study.

❑ Point out a trend and link it to your topic.

❑ Provide a self-test.

❑ Write a "100 Days To . . ." type of e-mail–based coaching program.

❑ Tell a story.

❑ Include your signature (with contact info).

❑ Offer a discussion list for readers to join if desired.

4. WRITE YOUR E-NEWSLETTER / TIP WELL

❑ Write snappy titles: exact, simple, surprising, direct.

❑ Use metaphors and analogies.

❑ Make a distinction (A vs. B).

❑ Speak in messages that direct and guide the reader.

❑ Break your tip into three parts.

❑ Speak personally/conversationally vs. theoretically.

❑ Be jargon-free (or else explain it).

❑ Use very specific words.

❑ Ask yourself "What do I want the reader to know most?"

❑ Ask for feedback from readers in order to improve your style.

5. MARKETING / BUILDING SUBSCRIBERS

❑ E-mail your first issue to everyone you know.

❑ Add a "how to subscribe" segment at the beginning and end.

❑ Let visitors to your site subscribe from your site.

❑ List your newsletter/tips at mailing list websites.

❑ Get your newsletter/tips announced via Scout.

❑ Write provocative, rich, opinionated copy that gets passed around.

❑ Offer and encourage liberal retransmittal/ reproduction rights.

❑ Swap announcements with other list owners.

❑ Offer more than one tip/news broadcast to accommodate multiple markets.

❑ Purchase opt-in subscriber lists and market to these.

6. BROADCAST MANAGEMENT SYSTEMS & FEATURES

❑ After one hundred subscribers, automate the sub/unsubscribe process with majordomo, listserv, or LetterRip (programs accessed on the Internet which help to automate the subscription process).

❑ After 500 subscribers, start offering a daily tip.

❑ After 500 subscribers, use a broadcast queuing/ hopper system to allow you to prepare your issues in advance.

❑ After 1,000 subscribers, start queuing your plugs/ marketing messages.

❑ After 1,000 subscribers, offer a second e-mail list using a single database.

❑ After 1,000 subscribers, add a system that will automatically delete your e-mail.

❑ Let subscribers receive single e-mail–digest of multiple tips/newsletters.

❑ Add a feature that lets you send out sequential e-mails (for a step-by-step course).

❑ After 5,000 subscribers, hire a broadcast manager.

❑ Automatically post your tips/newsletters to your website.

7. MAKING MONEY WITH YOUR E-NEWSLETTER / TIP BROADCAST

❑ Offer a book, audiotape, or audiotape set.

❑ Offer free TeleClasses (10-20 percent will convert to clients to pay for classes).

❑ Offer fee-based TeleClasses (1 percent of subscribers will sign up).

❑ Plug a colleague (and then they can plug you).

❑ Sell other people's books, programs, diagnostic tools, products, and services.

❑ Convert your topic into a web-based course.

❑ Sell advertising (if your list gets to 10,000 or more subscribers).

❑ Create an online community and offer them branded products.

❑ Help others write/package their content into newsletters.

From *The Coaching Starter Kit* by CoachVille.com, published by W.W. Norton & Company, Inc.
Form courtesy of and copyrighted by Thomas Leonard

8. KEY SUCCESS STRATEGIES

❑ Offer a daily tip versus just a weekly newsletter.

❑ Have more than just one tip/newsletter.

❑ If you can't write well, learn how to or hire someone.

❑ Create corresponding services to accompany your tip/newsletter topic.

❑ Keep experimenting with topics/subjects until you find one that people subscribe to in droves.

❑ After 1,000 subscribers, convert your tip e-zine into a virtual community.

❑ Don't give up; critical mass is at 5,000 subscribers.

❑ Don't expect immediate revenue, but it will come.

❑ Pick a topic that people want, not just what you think is interesting.

❑ Target market segments/industry groups given the high referral rate.

9. TOPICS TO WRITE ABOUT

❑ Relationships (finding and improving).

❑ Career (advancement and transition).

❑ Small business (entrepreneurship and making money).

❑ Living well (fulfillment and happiness).

❑ Professional success (marketing and practice management).

❑ Skills (communication and technical).

❑ Internet (marketing and cyber skills).

❑ Personal development (self-improvement and spirituality).

❑ Self-care (nutrition and balance).

❑ Market segments (women, men, parents, etc.).

10. TURN YOUR NEWSLETTER INTO A COMMUNITY / NETWORK

❑ Come up with a community name versus just a newsletter's name.

❑ Provide a directory of all subscribers who wish to be listed.

❑ Offer special get-togethers or free services to members.

❑ Group members with similar classified listings in your newsletter.

❑ Offer discussions for subgroups of your subscribers.

❑ Offer special discounts to your subscribers.

❑ Turn your readers into your research and development team for program development.

❑ Offer prizes and gifts for their input/help/ideas.

❑ Set up local meetings/chapters for subscribers to meet each other.

❑ Find out what your community wants and then offer it to them.

From *The Coaching Starter Kit* by CoachVille.com, published by W. W. Norton & Company, Inc.
Form courtesy of and copyrighted by Thomas Leonard

Certified Cyber: Internet-Related Skills That Everyone Should Have

1. E-MAIL BASICS

- I have an e-mail program (AOL, Outlook Express, Eudora, Communicator).
- I can send e-mail to 1 person at a time.
- I can send e-mail to 50 people at a time.
- I can send a carbon copy (cc) to one person.
- I can cc 50 people.
- I can send a blind carbon copy (bcc) to 1 person.
- I can send a bcc to 50 people.
- I can adjust my "reply-to" address.
- My 'from' e-mail address is correct.
- My name is included in the 'from' e-mail address.

2. E-MAIL—INTERMEDIATE

- My signature is at the end of my e-mails.
- I can reply to a sender and include their original e-mail.
- I can insert my reply in the body of the sender's e-mail.
- I know how to reply to both the sender and the other cc'd parties.
- I can attach a word or text document.
- I can attach a gif or jpg file.
- I know about not using CAPS.
- I have used an e-mail autoresponder.
- I can cut and paste from a document into an e-mail.
- I know about web-based e-mail.

3. E-MAIL—ADVANCED

- I know about ASCII versus HTML e-mail.
- I can change the color of the e-mail text.
- I can change size of e-mail text.

- I can change style of the e-mail text.
- My e-mail system keeps copies of my sent e-mails.
- I can delete my sent e-mails once a week.
- I can delete my deleted e-mails weekly.
- I know how to adjust my e-mail system to send the message right away or to wait.
- I can include e-mail addresses of my friends and colleagues in an e-mail–based address book.
- I know how to attach an audio or video file to my e-mail message.

4. RECEIVING E-MAIL

- I know about my encryption options. I have set up folders to file/organize my incoming e-mails.
- I have set up filters to direct my incoming mail into folders.
- I know where on my hard drive my attached files are downloaded/saved to.
- I know how to set up my e-mail system to check for multiple e-mail accounts.
- I know how to open several/all incoming messages at once.
- I know how to sort my e-mail by date, topic, or sender.
- I've set up my computer to check for mail automatically.
- I know how to include the sender's e-mail when I click "reply."
- I don't let unanswered e-mails pile up.

5. BROWSER—BASICS

- I have the current version of my browser.
- I know how to flush my browser cache.
- I can bookmark my favorite websites.

From *The Coaching Starter Kit* by CoachVille.com, published by W. W. Norton & Company, Inc.

217

- I can use the back and forward buttons.
- I can open more than one window.
- I know how to set the page my browser goes to when it starts up.
- I know how to read the raw HTML of a web page using the View Source button.
- I know how to reload/refresh a browser.
- I've set the search page button to go to the search engine of my choice.
- I've set my downloading preferences.

6. BROWSER—INTERMEDIATE

- QuickTime Player is installed.
- RealPlayer is installed.
- Vivo Plug-in is installed.
- Acrobat Reader is installed.
- Shockwave Plug-in is installed
- Flash Player is installed.
- I've set up a personalized homepage at yahoo or elsewhere.
- I've searched using the major search engines.
- I can view PDFs via my browser.

7. WEB SURFING

- I know how to enter a passcoded area.
- I know about cookies. I know when not to use an online form.
- I know how to subscribe to an e-mail newsletter via majordomo.
- I know how to download a file.
- I've participated in web-based chat.
- I've used web-based telephone.
- I know I have to install newly downloaded software before I can use it.

- I can install downloaded software.

8. SOFTWARE / EQUIPMENT

- I have the latest version of a word processing program for a MAC or PC.
- I have the latest versions of Photoshop, PaintShop, or PhotoDeluxe.
- I have backup software.
- I have speakers and a microphone.
- I have an ergonomic keyboard.
- I have a scanner.
- I have a fast, high-quality color printer.
- I have a tape backup system or zip drive.
- I have a UPS battery backup/surge protector.

9. GENERAL WEB / COMPUTER

- I back up my hard drive at least weekly.
- I have a QuickCam with which I can take videos and pictures.
- I know how to upload files via FTP.
- I know how to create web pages/HTML.
- I have a computer expert or friend who can answer my questions right away.
- I know about automatically backing up my key files via the web.
- I get my news, quotes, and tips sent to me each day via e-mail.
- I automatically connect to my ISP when I launch my browser or e-mail.
- I have upgraded to ADSL or cable.
- I know how to view a gif or jpg file on my hard drive by using my browser.

From *The Coaching Starter Kit* by CoachVille.com, published by W.W. Norton & Company, Inc.

Chapter 8

Event Planning and Evaluation

EVENTS
Event Preparation Short Survey

Fill in the spaces below.

Name of event:_____

Date of the event: _____ Time: _____

Description of event (reception, lunch, dinner): _____

Where will the event take place? _____

Who is the host of the event?_____

What is the purpose of the event? Is there a reception before/after the event? _____

Will alcohol be served? _____

How many people are expected? _____

How many presenters will there be?_____

How much time has been set aside for each presenter? _____

Will there be someone presenting the speaker? _____

Who? _____

Who is the audience (as a group)? _____

Can you name a few of the participants and their occupations? _____

Contact person responsible for organizing the details: _____

Name: _____ Tel #: _____

Will a projector be available for a computer hookup?_____

Is there a podium? _____

Height?_____ Lectern?_____

Will a lapel FM microphone be available? _____

Trade Fair / Event Checklist

DISPLAY ITEMS TO BRING	PERSON SUPPLYING
Table cloth	
Computer and display program(s)	
Screen and data show projector	
Extension cords and computer peripherals as appropriate	
Interactive displays	
Business cards and bowl to collect visitor cards	
Posters and displays	
Signs, flowers, balloons, etc.	
Gifts, giveaways, brochures	
Photographs, testimonials, and news items to display	
Activity invitations to attract prospects	
Diary, notepad	
Chair	
Drinks and snacks	
Someone to assist you!!	

From *The Coaching Starter Kit* by CoachVille.com, published by W. W. Norton & Company, Inc.
Form courtesy of and copyrighted by Coach Wendy Whittem-Trunz

WORKSHOPS
Workshop Setup Checklist

Date: _____

Venue: _____

Attendees: _____

Room	previous day/evening—set up room/check
	charge copier batteries
	ensure all supplies are available
	set up coffee, etc.

Equipment	(electronic) white board & extra paper—clean eraser
	white board copier & extra paper
	notebook computer
	datashow projector
	overhead projector
	extension cords, adapters, etc.
	screen
	TV & video
	flip chart & paper
	posters
	camera & film
	pens/pencils/overhead pens
	whiteboard markers
	bulldog clips, blue tack, tape, etc.
	tape player & music
	program tapes, videos
	toys, music as required

Material & Paperwork	client file
	diagnostic report
	workshop facilitator's guidelines & materials
	workshop plan file prepared in advance
	workshop agenda overhead or copy
	other (blank) overheads as required
	workbooks as required
	worksheets
	other—ice breakers, activities, etc

From *The Coaching Starter Kit* by CoachVille.com, published by W.W. Norton & Company, Inc.
Form courtesy of and copyrighted by Coach Wendy Whittem-Trunz

Workshop Feedback

Check and fill in the blanks where appropriate.

Speaker: _____ Excellent _____ Good _____ Fair _____ Poor
Location: _____ Excellent _____ Good _____ Fair _____ Poor
Comments: _____

_____

_____

_____

_____

_____

_____

_____

_____

_____

_____

_____

LOOKING FOR ADDITIONAL SUPPORT?

____ I would like to receive your monthly newsletter filled with tips on business building, coaching, etc.

My e-mail address is: _____

____ I would like to receive your monthly e-mail newsletter on coaching.

My e-mail address is: _____

____ I would like to take you up on a free session of coaching, so I can see if it would be of value to me.

____ I would like to take you up on a free consultation to see how bringing coaching into my business or organization could produce more results.

____ I would like to be notified of other coaching events.

____ I would like you to speak at my group/organization meeting.

Name: _____

Address: _____

Phone: _____ Fax: _____

Date of birth: _____

From *The Coaching Starter Kit* by CoachVille.com, published by W. W. Norton & Company, Inc.
Form courtesy of and copyrighted by Kenneth Abrams

CONFERENCES
Conference Venue Quote Request

Venue	
Venue requirements	

Room name
   Size
   Seating
	_____ # attendees; _____ # facilitators/coaches

Date and time	
Equipment and supplies	electronic white board and plenty of paper and pens projector and screen TV and VCR photocopier to copy transparencies flip charts fax machine lectern and microphone

Refreshments
   Breakfast
   Morning and afternoon tea
   Lunch
   Dinner
   and special diet requests
	served/buffet—menu fixed or options

Contact person(s) and title	
Phone and fax	
E-mail address	
Confirmation by:	

Other information:
   Parking
   Deposit
   Cancellation policy	

Total cost and breakdown	

From *The Coaching Starter Kit* by CoachVille.com, published by W.W. Norton & Company, Inc.
Form courtesy of and copyrighted by Coach Wendy Whittem-Trunz

Seminar Evaluation

Content: *Please circle the number that reflects your opinion.*

1. Not at all   2. To a small extent   3. To a moderate extent   4. To a great extent   5. Very much

To what extent did the seminar meet your objectives?	1	2	3	4	5
How well did the seminar match the description?	1	2	3	4	5
How applicable is this seminar content to your life?	1	2	3	4	5
How would you rate the overall pace of the seminar?	1	2	3	4	5
How useful were the handouts?	1	2	3	4	5

Comments _____

_____

_____

_____

Seminar Leader: *Please circle the number that reflects your opinion.*

1. Poor   2. Below average   3. Average   4. Above average   5. Excellent

The leader's presentation style of the material was	1	2	3	4	5
The leader's knowledge of the subject was	1	2	3	4	5
The organization of the material was	1	2	3	4	5
The leader's ability to stimulate group participation was	1	2	3	4	5

Comments _____

_____

_____

_____

_____

_____

What additional resources would help you in your personal and professional life? _____

_____

_____

Would you like to learn more about upcoming seminars or teleclasses?   ❑ Yes   ❑ No

From *The Coaching Starter Kit* by CoachVille.com, published by W.W. Norton & Company, Inc.
Form courtesy of and copyrighted by Maria Marsala
Original version of this form by Coach Cynthia Stringer

What other topics are of interest to you? _____

_____

_____

Would you like to schedule a complimentary coaching session? If yes, what is the best time to call you? _____

_____

_____

Send me a complimentary copy of your online newsletter. Print your e-mail address here: _____

_____

_____

_____

DO YOU BELONG TO A GROUP OR ASSOCIATION LOOKING FOR A SPEAKER? IF YES, COMPLETE AS MUCH OF THE FOLLOWING INFORMATION AS POSSIBLE.

Name of group _____ Date speaker needed _____

Subject_____ Contact _____

Contact information_____

What was the best, usable idea you gained from today's program? How do you plan to use the information? What do you wish there had been more time for? _____

_____

_____

May I quote you?   ❑ Yes   ❑ No

PLEASE FILL OUT THIS INFORMATION TO BE PLACED ON OUR MAILING LIST AND TO FIND OUT ABOUT UPCOMING WORKSHOPS.

Name _____

Address_____

City _____

State_____ Zip _____

Phone _____

Please print e-mail _____

Company/profession _____

From *The Coaching Starter Kit* by CoachVille.com, published by W. W. Norton & Company, Inc
Form courtesy of and copyrighted by Maria Marsala
Original version of this form by Coach Cynthia Stringer

Part 4

For Your Client

Chapter 9

Basic Client Worksheets

WHAT IS COACHING?

Coaching is a newer profession, which has synthesized the best from psychology, business, evolution, philosophy, spirituality, and finance to benefit individuals and groups.

WHY DOES COACHING WORK?

Coaching works because of three unique features:

Synergy

Client and coach become a team, focusing on the client's goals and needs and accomplishing more than the client would alone.

Structure

With a coach, a client takes more actions, thinks bigger, and gets the job done thanks to the accountability provided by the coach.

Expertise

The coach knows how to help entrepreneurs earn more money, make better decisions, set the best goals, and restructure their professional and personal lives for maximum productivity.

WHO WORKS WITH A COACH?

Entrepreneurs, business owners, professionals, and people in transition use a coach to create, plan, or solve something, personally and/or professionally.

WHAT IS WORKED ON?

Here is what the client and coach work on together:

- Business planning, budgeting, and goal-setting
- Balancing business and personal life
- Maximizing work effort
- Handling business or personal problems
- Making key decisions and designing strategies
- Prioritizing actions and projects
- Catching up and getting ahead of the business
- Training, developing, and managing staff
- Increasing sales substantially, or filling a practice
- Turning around a difficult situation

From *The Coaching Starter Kit* by CoachVille.com, published by W. W. Norton & Company, Inc.

BUT HOW DOES A COACH DO THIS?

Coaching is delivered during regular, weekly sessions by telephone and/or in person, whichever is more convenient. Clients bring an agenda of items to the call. The coach helps them to solve problems and make the most of opportunities. When they are taking on a large goal, coaches help them design the project and provide the support and structure needed to make sure it gets done. Coaches bring out the client's best by offering advice, expecting a lot, helping them strategize, and celebrating the wins.

WHAT SHOULD I LOOK FOR IN A COACH?

The right coach brings out your best, consistently. To do this, the coach you select should pass the following three tests:

1. Does this coach have a track record of helping someone like me accomplish the goals I want?
2. Do I feel good and motivated to act with this coach?
3. Will this coach keep up with me—and ahead of me—as I grow? You can always check references and try out the coach for a month to see if he or she is really the right one for you.

HOW MUCH DOES IT COST?

The fee for most entrepreneur and professional clients ranges from $200 to $500 per month for a weekly meeting or coaching call. My monthly coaching fee is $ _____ for a weekly half-hour call or $ _____ for a weekly one-hour call, using my 800 number. There are no other charges and clients may phone in between calls for additional assistance, if needed. (For projects, I bill at $ _____ per hour. For presentations, facilitating, or training, the fee is $ _____ per day, plus expenses).

HOW WOULD I GET STARTED?

If you feel that this type of relationship could work for you, call a coach and talk. Coaching is not something we sell; it is something you buy because you want it.

WHERE DO I START WITH A COACH?

Most coaches begin with a special client meeting to get to know one another. The coach wants to hear about the client's goals, needs, and problems. The client wants to get comfortable with the coach. During this meeting, both parties design a list of goals and a game plan to reach these goals. Prior to this meeting, the client will have received a welcome package of checklists and assessment materials to make the most of the meeting. Coaches often spend extra time (gratis) with new clients getting to know them and coaching them to set the best goals for themselves. Together coaches and clients design the best way to work as a team to accomplish their goals.

The Professional Coach Is...

- Your partner in achieving business and personal goals

- Your champion during a turnaround

- Your trainer in communication and life skills

- Your sounding board when making choices

- Your motivation when strong actions are called for

- Your unconditional support when you take a hit

- Your mentor in personal development

- Your co-designer when creating an extraordinary project

- Your beacon during stormy times

- Your wake-up call if you don't hear your own

and most importantly...

- The professional coach is your partner in helping you have all of what matters most to you.

From *The Coaching Starter Kit* by CoachVille.com, published by W.W. Norton & Company, Inc.
Form courtesy of and copyrighted by Thomas Leonard

Coaching Focus Areas

What would you like to work on?

PERSONAL FOCI

- ❏ Financial stress/problem
- ❏ Personal organization
- ❏ Happiness/fulfillment
- ❏ Communication skills
- ❏ Personal evolution
- ❏ Relationship problems
- ❏ Relationship enhancement
- ❏ Life purpose clarification
- ❏ Salary/income
- ❏ Stress reduction
- ❏ Personal life plan design
- ❏ Blocks/obstacle removal
- ❏ Spiritual development
- ❏ Time management
- ❏ Internet/cyber skills
- ❏ Decision-making
- ❏ Adrenaline reduction
- ❏ Motivation/inspiration
- ❏ Structure/support
- ❏ Problem resolution
- ❏ Balance improvement
- ❏ Career change/transition
- ❏ Career advancement
- ❏ Goal identification
- ❏ Setting priorities
- ❏ Personal foundation
- ❏ Values clarification
- ❏ Needs identification
- ❏ Needs satisfaction
- ❏ Toleration reduction

- ❏ Self-care skills
- ❏ Truth identification
- ❏ Family communication
- ❏ Increase awareness
- ❏ Creativity/innovation skills
- ❏ Legacy identification
- ❏ Acceptance of events
- ❏ Acceptance of others
- ❏ Increase learning rate
- ❏ Stronger boundaries
- ❏ Higher standards
- ❏ Grace/style development
- ❏ Compassion/empathy
- ❏ Reserves/security increase
- ❏ Confidence
- ❏ Integrity improvement
- ❏ Fear/resistance reduction
- ❏ Life simplification
- ❏ Character development
- ❏ Communication skills
- ❏ Strengths identification
- ❏ Passion identification
- ❏ Peace/harmony
- ❏ Selfishness/pleasure
- ❏ Receptiveness/flexibility
- ❏ Self-awareness
- ❏ Personal turnaround
- _____
- _____
- _____
- _____
- _____
- _____

BUSINESS FOCI

- ❏ Revenue growth
- ❏ Profit growth
- ❏ Value added for customers
- ❏ Productivity/effectiveness
- ❏ New business start-up
- ❏ Marketing plan
- ❏ Internet marketing
- ❏ Team/collaboration
- ❏ Project management
- ❏ Product quality
- ❏ Negotiation skills
- ❏ Professional networking
- ❏ Marketing training
- ❏ Vision/mission
- ❏ Internet/cyber skills
- ❏ Management skills
- ❏ Reputation development
- ❏ Employee retention
- ❏ New economy orientation
- ❏ New client acquisition
- ❏ Leadership skills
- ❏ Improve staff morale
- ❏ Improve company culture
- ❏ Improve intangibles
- _____
- _____
- _____
- _____
- _____
- _____

From *The Coaching Starter Kit* by CoachVille.com, published by W. W. Norton & Company, Inc.

241

My Commitments & Coaching Preparation

At each coaching meeting, record your commitments for the next period.

Meeting #: _____ Date: _____

Name: _____ Attendees: _____

TASK	HELP BY	DUE	COMPLETE

Key achievements since our last coaching session _____

_____

What I have learned_____

_____

My reward is_____

_____

What I haven't achieved and why _____

_____

Questions and future challenges to address with coach_____

_____

From *The Coaching Starter Kit* by CoachVille.com, published by W. W. Norton & Company, Inc.
Form courtesy of and copyrighted by Coach Wendy Whittem-Trunz

Focus & Scope of Work

Please complete this and return to the coach. Be sure to include target dates for reaching each goal or objective. What are we going to work on together?

PERSONAL GOALS   **BY**

❏ _____

❏ _____

❏ _____

BUSINESS / PROFESSIONAL OBJECTIVES   **BY**

❏ _____

❏ _____

❏ _____

LIFE SKILLS   **BY**

❏ _____

❏ _____

❏ _____

COMMUNICATION SKILLS   **BY**

❏ _____

❏ _____

❏ _____

OTHER GOALS, DISTINCTIONS, AND CONDITIONS TO HAVE   **BY**

❏ _____

❏ _____

❏ _____

Promise Log

Write down the promises you make to yourself and your coach.

DATE MADE	DATE DUE	COMPLETED?	SPECIFIC PROMISE OR GOAL

From *The Coaching Starter Kit* by CoachVille.com, published by W. W. Norton & Company, Inc.

247

Coaching Session Prep Form #1

Please use this form to prepare for your coaching sessions and give it to your coach before each session.

1. What have been the wins for you in the past week?

   - ❑
   - ❑
   - ❑
   - ❑
   - ❑

2. What challenges did you experience this week? How did you handle them? What have been the opportunities for growth or evolution?

   - ❑
   - ❑
   - ❑
   - ❑
   - ❑

3. What would you like to accomplish in the next week regarding the goals you set for coaching? What can we talk about during our call to move you toward those goals?

   Goal #1:

   Discussion Focus:

   Goal #2:

   Discussion Focus:

   Goal #3:

   Discussion Focus:

4. What else would you like to talk about, which has come up or come to you?

   - ❑
   - ❑
   - ❑
   - ❑
   - ❑

From *The Coaching Starter Kit* by CoachVille.com, published by W.W. Norton & Company, Inc.
Form courtesy of and copyrighted by Rinatta Paries, Relationship Coach

Coaching Session Prep Form #2

Please respond to each question in the space provided.

WHAT I HAVE ACCOMPLISHED SINCE OUR LAST CALL

❑ _____
❑ _____
❑ _____

WHAT I DIDN'T ACCOMPLISH, BUT INTENDED TO

❑ _____
❑ _____
❑ _____

THE CHALLENGES AND PROBLEMS I AM FACING NOW

❑ _____
❑ _____
❑ _____

THE OPPORTUNITIES WHICH ARE AVAILABLE TO ME RIGHT NOW

❑ _____
❑ _____
❑ _____

I WANT TO USE THE COACH DURING THE CALL TO

❑ _____
❑ _____
❑ _____

WHAT I PROMISE TO DO BY THE NEXT CALL

❑ _____
❑ _____
❑ _____

From *The Coaching Starter Kit* by CoachVille.com, published by W. W. Norton & Company, Inc.

251

Coaching Session Discussion Topics

Because each coaching relationship is unique, it helps to know what is best to talk about during calls or meetings, and what not to talk about.

HOW ARE YOU?

- ❑ How you are feeling about yourself—good and bad
- ❑ How you are looking at your life
- ❑ How do you feel about others

WHAT HAS HAPPENED SINCE THE LAST CALL?

- ❑ What have you experienced since the last call
- ❑ Shifts, wins, and insights
- ❑ Any new choices or decisions made?
- ❑ Personal news

WHAT ARE YOU WORKING ON?

- ❑ Progress report on your goals, projects, and activities
- ❑ What you've done that you are proud of
- ❑ What you are coming up against

HOW I CAN HELP?

- ❑ Where you are stuck
- ❑ Where you are wondering about something
- ❑ A distinction
- ❑ A plan of action or strategy
- ❑ Some advice

WHAT IS NEXT?

- ❑ What is the next goal or project to take on
- ❑ What is the next goal or distinction to understand
- ❑ What do you want for yourself next

From *The Coaching Starter Kit* by CoachVille.com, published by W. W. Norton & Company, Inc.

253

I want you to benefit greatly from the time we have together each week and also during the time in between our calls. This brief guide is what most of my clients do to maximize the value from their coaching with me.

MAKE A LIST OF WHAT YOU REALLY WANT IN LIFE

Coaching works best when you have clear goals based on your needs and values. If you're not sure what your goals should be, we can discuss them during our call or session.

GET TO KNOW YOURSELF NEWLY

Working with a sensitive and empathic coach is a healthy way to grow. Most clients hire a coach to accomplish several specific goals and much of the time and focus is on these goals. Yet, don't be surprised if you discover new parts of yourself and adjust your goals accordingly. This discovery process is natural, so you needn't rush it, just realize it will likely happen. Accelerated personal and professional growth is the hallmark of being coached.

DOUBLE YOUR LEVEL OF WILLINGNESS

Part of working with me as your coach is that I will ask a lot of you—more than you may have been asked recently. I need you to be willing to experiment with fresh approaches and be open to redesigning the parts of your life that you are able to right now. This will help you to more easily reach your goals and live an integrated and fulfilled personal and professional life, using the gifts you have and enjoying life as it was meant to be enjoyed.

Please be willing to:

- ❑ Change your behavior
- ❑ Reassess the assumptions/decisions you've made
- ❑ Experiment
- ❑ Start telling what's really true
- ❑ Remove all sources of stress
- ❑ Eliminate all triggers of adrenaline
- ❑ Redesign how you spend your time
- ❑ Get the support you need to handle a problem
- ❑ Set bigger goals
- ❑ Raise your personal standards
- ❑ Start treating people better
- ❑ Stop tolerating or suffering from your life

Please make a list of the ten things you are now willing to do or change.

From *The Coaching Starter Kit* by CoachVille.com, published by W. W. Norton & Company, Inc.
Form courtesy of and copyrighted by Linda Mitchell, Coaches For Life

COME TO THE COACHING CALL PREPARED, WITH AN AGENDA

We have thirty minutes together and you'll want to have a written list of things to share and discuss. On this list, include elements like:

❑ Success and wins that you've had that week

❑ Report on the homework

❑ Problems you faced/how you handled them

❑ Advice you want about a situation

❑ What you're currently working on/how it's going

❑ New skills you want to develop

❑ Insights and new awarenesses

❑ Strategies you wish to develop

ENJOY YOUR SESSION

We have work to do together, clearly, but feel free to enjoy the session. After several sessions, you may find that we take a little time to catch up on those parts of your life that mean a lot to you, or you may want to share something personal and confidential. And after several months (perhaps sooner), you may find that we even laugh during the call—at life, how you've grown, how things happen. Coaching calls aren't gabfests, but they are enjoyable. They needn't be intense or an effort for you to produce the miracles you know are possible. Feel free to set the tone of the calls and I will respect what you need in this area.

WORK THE OTHER PROGRAMS OF YOUR CHOICE

You are invited to work on any of the forms and programs I have for my clients:

❑ 10 Keys to Time Management

❑ Resources and Assets

❑ Special Project

❑ Current Status Evaluation

❑ Life Purpose Worksheet

❑ Action Plan

Select one or two which most appeal to you and let's work on these together.

From *The Coaching Starter Kit* by CoachVille.com, published by W.W. Norton & Company, Inc.

KEEP YOURSELF WELL BETWEEN SESSIONS

Coaching can require energy; emotionally, intellectually, and physically. Given this, take extraordinary care of your health and emotional balance while being coached. The place to start is to develop a list of ten daily habits which keep you well. Some of the habits my clients have developed into a routine are:

- ❑ Exercise
- ❑ Reduce fat intake
- ❑ Read
- ❑ Listen to great music
- ❑ Meditate
- ❑ Underpromise, don't overextend yourself
- ❑ Handle unresolved matters
- ❑ No caffeine/nicotine/alcohol
- ❑ Start being early
- ❑ Limit sugar intake
- ❑ Take vitamins
- ❑ Write in your journal

DO YOUR HOMEWORK EACH WEEK

These are tasks, actions, results, or changes you are telling yourself and your coach that you will do your best to complete before your next session. You must apply yourself and use the homework to help you achieve your personal and business goals.

From *The Coaching Starter Kit* by CoachVille.com, published by W. W. Norton & Company, Inc.

Top 10 Ways to Get the Most out of Your Coaching

Just by having a coach and chatting with him/her on a regular basis, you will reap the benefits of coaching. The synergy that occurs as a result of the coach/client relationship is what makes the biggest difference to any well-motivated client.

But if you want to maximize the value of the coaching relationship, here are ten ways to do so that I have seen work very, very well. If some of the ideas are new to you, we can talk about them in our first several sessions.

1. **Focus on how you feel and want to feel, not just on what you want to produce**

   Sometimes, clients feel the need to focus their coaching time on how to produce more tangible results; but do not forget the intangibles such as feeling happier, more peaceful, and more inspired. Results are very important, but the feelings you experience during your day are equally important. Think of a brick wall—the bricks are the results, the mortar is the feelings. Enjoy having both.

2. **Talk about what matters most to you**

   You may talk about anything you want during the coaching session. This includes your goals, your life, your needs, what you want to improve, what's bothering you, an idea you have, a problem you are dealing with, even issues that may not appear to be all that useful to talk about. It's surprising what a difference it makes in the long run when you focus on what you most selfishly want to talk about during coaching, not what you feel you should talk about.

3. **Sensitize yourself to see and experience things earlier than before**

   As you know, time is collapsing, meaning that things are happening faster and faster and the pace of change continues to increase. For some, this causes stress because they feel both the pressure to keep up and the fear of getting left behind. But for others, they recognize this phenomenon as a chance to seize opportunities. How does one do this? Reduce whatever clouds your ability to see or numbs your ability to sense; we call this process "sensitizing yourself." The more you can feel, the faster you can respond to events and opportunities. You sensitize yourself by reducing or eliminating alcohol, television, adrenaline, stress, and caffeine.

4. **Feel coached during the 10,000 minutes of your week, not just the 30 minutes of your session**

   There are 10,080 minutes in a week. Coaching occurs during your entire week, not just during your coaching session—such is the power of coaching and the coaching relationship. What you and your coach talk about during your sessions will resonate with you during your week, and some of the seeds or ideas that were discussed will grow between sessions. All you have to do is to live your life fully between coaching sessions and be open to seeing what you and your coach talked about.

From *The Coaching Starter Kit* by CoachVille.com, published by W. W. Norton & Company, Inc.
Form courtesy of and copyrighted by Thomas Leonard

5. Reduce the drain and strain on your life

Coaching works because it focuses you on two life areas: First, you will be helped to stretch yourself further, take more actions than you would on your own, and devise/implement effective strategies to get what you want. Second, you will also be identifying and reducing areas of stress, such as tolerations, stressful situations, difficult relationships, pressured environments, and recurring problems. So, don't just hoist a bigger sail, make sure there are no cracks or barnacles on your hull.

6. Get more space, not just time, in your life

Coaching needs room in order to work. If you are too busy, rushed, or burdened, you will be using coaching to push yourself even harder, instead of using coaching to become more effective. We strongly suggest that you put some projects on hold, reduce your goals, simplify your day, streamline your work, before or immediately after starting with a coach. Simplification gives you space. Space is needed to learn and evolve beyond where you are today.

7. Become incredibly selfish

Coaching is about you and what you most want. As such, you will probably need to start putting yourself first if you haven't done so already. At the very least, you will want to become selfish, in the sense that *you* are what matters most. When you are happy and doing well, others will benefit as well.

8. Be open to seeing things differently

In coaching, you will work with your goals and strategize to reach these goals. But you will also be working on you. In other words, you will get more out of coaching if you are willing to relook at some of your assumptions, ways of thinking, expectations, beliefs, reactions, and approaches to success. There are always newly developed concepts, principles, distinctions, and evolutionary steps to learn. You will not be forced or even encouraged to make these changes given they are so personal, but we do ask that you at least consider different approaches and try them out to see if they work for you.

9. Be willing to evolve, not just develop

Coaching is both a developmental process as well as an evolutionary one. In other words, you will be learning how to accomplish more with less effort—let's call this the developmental aspect of coaching. But you will also be thinking differently and expanding yourself and your world, which we call evolving. Evolving is a skill worth learning because life itself is evolving, not just developing.

10. Design and strengthen your personal and business environments

The value of coaching can be extended if you take time to design the perfect environment in which to live and work. Where you live and how you live are key to your success. Who you spend time with and who inspires can make the difference between success and failure. Be willing to invest some time in improving your surroundings so that you feel supported to be your best.

From *The Coaching Starter Kit* by CoachVille.com, published by W.W. Norton & Company, Inc.
Form courtesy of and copyrighted by Thomas Leonard

6 Benefits of Working with a Coach

Coaching is proven to work when two factors are present:

1. The client is willing to grow

2. There is a gap between where he/she is now and where he/she wants to be.

That is all that is necessary for you and your coach to solve problems, create a new life, turn a business around, double sales and profitability, and design and implement a plan of action. Or, whatever else is called for to ensure that you have what you need to get more of what you want.

WITH A COACH, YOU WILL:

1. **Take more, better, and smarter action**
   Because you set the goals you really want

   Our first task together is to find out exactly what you want for yourself. Once you create objectives that are clearly in line with your personal values and professional vision, you are much more likely to naturally and consistently take actions to reach them.

2. **Have a balanced life**
   Because you designed it

   Professional success is maximized when you enjoy a sense of personal fulfillment and life balance. We will discuss how to be selfish yet responsible, and how to carve out enough time so your life outside of work is exactly the way you want it to be.

3. **Make and keep more money**
   You are worth more than you're making

   Most people are worth more than they are making. Are you happy with your financial situation? If not, you and your coach can look at your beliefs about money and address whatever is keeping you from experiencing financial abundance.

4. **Reach for more, much more**
   And not be consumed in the process

   When you have a partner you trust, you will reach for much more because you can afford to. Are you ready to think big and really live your life fully? A coach is a partner who will enable you to take your life wherever you want it to go.

5. **Make better decisions for yourself and your business**
   Because your focus is clear

   Your coach will help you become focused as you share ideas with him/her. A coach will understand you and be subjective enough to want a lot for you, yet objective enough to not be biased or self-serving. Just talking about your options with someone who really listens is often not enough to clarify things.

6. **Have a lot more sustainable energy**
   No more chugging along

   Your coach will help you to identify the things that drain your energy and create a long-term strategy to eliminate them. In addition, your coach will focus on the things that give you energy and explore how to maximize their impact. When you're happy, productive, and free from tolerations and problems, life is a lot more fun!

The Success Process:
10 Steps to Sustainable, Fulfilling Success

1. **Stop tolerating**

   When you stop putting up with stuff, you will have more energy.

2. **Get complete**

   When you complete unfinished business and fully communicate, you will experience peace.

3. **Simplify everything**

   When you simplify your life, you will have much more space, and experience balance.

4. **Strengthen your foundation**

   When your needs are met and your personal foundation is solid, confidence replaces fear.

5. **Orient yourself around what matters**

   When your life is oriented around what is most important to you, you will have clarity about what's next.

6. **Experiment and improve, continuously**

   When you try new things or ways of thinking, you will become a more creative person.

7. **Improve your strengths**

   When you build on what you have, you will become more successful.

8. **Stockpile**

   When you build a reserve in every area, you can leverage more opportunities more quickly.

9. **Integrate your life**

   When you make sure your life's components fit together well, you will experience effortlessness.

10. **Polish everything**

    When you buff up every aspect of your life, you will feel even more proud.

From *The Coaching Starter Kit* by CoachVille.com, published by W. W. Norton & Company, Inc.

19 Evolutionary Practices

Want to evolve yourself? Here's what to do.

Personal evolution is distinct from personal development. When you evolve, you alter. When you develop, you become more of who you are. Both are excellent approaches to a rich and fulfilling life, but they are different enough that a coach should know which their clients are experiencing.

1. **Surround yourself with new ideas instead of recycling your beliefs**
   Beliefs can limit your ability to experience life as it unfolds.

2. **Seek out chaos whenever you can**
   The unexpected is necessary for survival in a rapidly changing world.

3. **Be aware of your surroundings**
   Evolution occurs as you respond to the stimuli in your environments.

4. **Use your tolerations to evolve how you operate**
   Every single thing you are putting up with is an opportunity waiting to be leveraged.

5. **Experiment constantly until you do so naturally and effortlessly**
   You may need to alter your relationship with risk in order to enjoy experimentation.

6. **Spend more time in nature**
   Nature nourishes and calibrates our natural systems.

7. **Become the host of a thriving network**
   Let your network evolve you as you invent clever ways to serve them.

8. **Continuously integrate all aspects of your life**
   Integration evolves you from being needlessly complicated to being richly complex.

9. **Actively choose and design your sources of energy**
   You can then operate at a higher, more effective frequency.

10. **Become superconductive**
    Reduce the energy you consume by 90 percent by decreasing your resistance to yourself, life, and events.

11. **Master the evolving set of cyber skills**
    Extend your intelligence by connecting with everyone and utilizing all aspects of the Internet.

12. **Surround yourself with people who are eagerly evolving**
    They spark you. You spark them. Evolution occurs naturally.

13. **Choose a goal or vision that is bigger than you are**
    Be pulled forward by it, instead of pushing yourself.

14. **Get over yourself in every possible way**
    Release the ego binds that keep you who you've been.

15. **Get to know every element of who you are and how you operate**
    This process of discovery and integration allows you to handle whatever comes up in life, so that you don't get waylaid by it.

16. **Take your gifts very, very seriously.**
    And design your life to fully develop and express them. Gifts are the levers of evolution.

17. **Emotionally heal, completely**
    Healing maximizes your emotional IQ and increases the rate at which you learn.

18. **Follow your whims**
    Whims are messages; develop the skill to read them.

19. **Make what you don't know more interesting than what you do know**
    Enjoy learning more than teaching.

From *The Coaching Starter Kit* by CoachVille.com, published by W. W. Norton & Company, Inc.
Form courtesy of and copyrighted by Thomas Leonard

SELF AND COACH EVALUATION
Are You Ready for Coaching?

If you are considering whether or not to hire a coach, you are deciding if you are ready to embark on a grand adventure. Coaching is not for everyone, and even highly coachable people have times in their lives when coaching may not be what they really want or need. Here are a few important questions to ask yourself before making your decision:

IS THIS THE RIGHT TIME FOR ME TO HIRE A COACH?

If you feel like you are ready to make some important changes, the time is right for you. If you are extremely busy and cannot imagine taking on another thing, then the answer is "probably yes." The first thing you and your coach may want to explore is what to remove from your busy schedule to make your life feel simpler, more balanced, and manageable.

CAN I AFFORD COACHING?

Make sure to look honestly at your finances before entering into the coaching relationship. If you hire a coach, you will be making an important investment in your life—equivalent in its overall impact to an advanced college degree. Are you able to pay the coach's fee for a minimum of six months without feeling like you are overextending yourself? If not, you may choose to continue, but work with your coach to improve your financial situation, immediately.

AM I WILLING TO TRY NEW THINGS?

During your coaching, you will be invited to look at old situations in new ways. You will be offered new concepts and different ways of approaching things. If you are willing to try out new possibilities and stretch your creative side, you will get a large return for your investment. If you are a person who vigorously defends your old perspectives, you will still get much value from committing yourself to a specific course of action.

IS COACHING WHAT I AM REALLY LOOKING FOR?

There are many other kinds of professional relationships, one of which might be more appropriate for you. Do you need an accountant, attorney, financial planner, or personal assistant? Your coach will certainly support you to find the right resources at the right time if you do. Just be aware that there may be additional expenses for professional services your coach is not qualified to provide for you. Are you experiencing chronic mental suffering or dwelling extensively on past events? If so, you probably want to talk to a therapist instead of—or in addition to— a coach. The idea is to build the kind of relationships that you *really* want and need.

From *The Coaching Starter Kit* by CoachVille.com, published by W. W. Norton & Company, Inc.
Form courtesy of and copyrighted by Damian Nash, Coach

Coaching Readiness Scale

Please provide your responses to the following statements: 1 (disagree) to 5 (strongly agree).

Name: _____

1. _____ I believe I am capable of having a life and career I truly desire.

2. _____ I am open to doing things in new and different ways to be successful.

3. _____ I am known for my courage, loyalty, integrity, and work ethic.

4. _____ I am an optimistic person.

5. _____ I am completely accountable for the results I produce.

6. _____ I have a clear view of where I am and where I want to go in life.

7. _____ I work well with others.

8. _____ I believe creating and sustaining relationships build strength.

9. _____ I live my life true to my values.

10. _____ I am willing to take the lead on issues that are important to me.

11. _____ I know I have unrealized potential.

12. _____ I am able to work outside my comfort zone.

13. _____ I have people in my life committed to my success.

14. _____ I want a very high quality of life.

15. _____ Producing quantifiable results is very important to me.

16. _____ I am a reliable person.

17. _____ Money is not the highest priority in my life.

18. _____ I am strongly committed to my personal development

19. _____ I am able to bounce back from setbacks.

20. _____ I am open to and welcome the contributions of others.

Scoring:
100–75	Excellent candidate for coaching; could see very good results
75–50	Good candidate for coaching; could see good results
50–25	Would benefit from coaching if willing to address hard issues; could see best results
25–0	Not yet a good candidate for coaching; needs to address commitment to personal success

From *The Coaching Starter Kit* by CoachVille.com, published by W. W. Norton & Company, Inc.
Form courtesy of and copyrighted by Linda Mitchell, Coaches For Life

Client Coachability Index

Circle the number that comes closest to representing how true the statement is for you right now. Then, score yourself using the key at the bottom of the page. Your coach needs for you to be at a place in life where you are coachable. This test helps him/her—and you—discover how coachable you are, right now.

NOT TRUE		TRUE			STATEMENT
1	2	3	4	5	I can be relied upon to be on time for all calls and appointments.
1	2	3	4	5	I am fully willing to do the work and let the coach do the coaching.
1	2	3	4	5	I keep my word without struggling or sabotaging.
1	2	3	4	5	I'll give the coach the benefit of the doubt and "try on" new concepts or different ways of doing things.
1	2	3	4	5	I will be truthful with the coach.
1	2	3	4	5	If I feel that I am not getting what I need or expect from the coach, I will share this as soon as I sense it and ask for what I want and need from the relationship.
1	2	3	4	5	I am willing to eliminate or modify the self-defeating behaviors which limit my success.
1	2	3	4	5	I have adequate funds to pay for coaching and will not regret or suffer about the fee. I see coaching as a worthwhile investment in my life.
1	2	3	4	5	I am someone who can share the credit for my success with the coach.

TOTAL SCORE (ADD UP ALL NUMBERS)

SCORING KEY

10–20   Not coachable right now.

21–30   Coachable, but make sure ground rules are honored!

31–40   Coachable.

41–50   Very coachable; ask the coach to ask a lot from you!

From *The Coaching Starter Kit* by CoachVille.com, published by W. W. Norton & Company, Inc.

Coaching Success Assessment

Please circle the appropriate number that best describes how you think and feel about your coaching relationship. The questions are either preceded by "My coach"... or followed by "... in our coaching relationship."

POINTS

DISAGREE			AGREE		COACHING ELEMENT
1	2	3	4	5	Identifies openings to performance, change, and transformation
1	2	3	4	5	Helps create a clear focus of coaching interaction during each session
1	2	3	4	5	Connects my development to an appropriate sense of urgency
1	2	3	4	5	Establishes clear priorities
1	2	3	4	5	Encourages me to take appropriate action through a planned, systemized process
1	2	3	4	5	Accountability is created around priorities and timelines
1	2	3	4	5	Offers to share experience and knowledge when appropriate
1	2	3	4	5	My coach has no authority, accountability, or responsibility for the outcomes
1	2	3	4	5	Takes time to learn about what I do in my job
1	2	3	4	5	I look forward to our meetings and interaction
1	2	3	4	5	Is available for prescheduled meetings and is accessible
1	2	3	4	5	The coaching time is free of interruption by outside influences
1	2	3	4	5	Information created during the interaction is valuable to my success
1	2	3	4	5	Coaching interaction is valuable to my performance and development
1	2	3	4	5	Explores the behaviors of others while valuing differences
1	2	3	4	5	Discusses my barriers to performance, change, and transformation
1	2	3	4	5	Always seems to notice how to acknowledge my efforts
1	2	3	4	5	Tells the truth, challenges, and encourages me without degrading me
1	2	3	4	5	Explains something, using clear and concise language—I know what is meant all the time
1	2	3	4	5	Continues to encourage my personal development throughout the coaching interaction
1	2	3	4	5	Is able to accept constructive criticism without getting defensive
1	2	3	4	5	The coaching interaction identifies my blind spots without prejudice or negative feedback
1	2	3	4	5	Is fun to be around and likable
1	2	3	4	5	Interaction is focused on creating opportunities
1	2	3	4	5	Makes an effort to understand how I personally feel about my situation
1	2	3	4	5	Hears what I say and what I don't say about issues we discuss

From *The Coaching Starter Kit* by CoachVille.com, published by W. W. Norton & Company, Inc.
Form courtesy of and copyrighted by W. Jan Austin

DISAGREE AGREE	COACHING ELEMENT
1 2 3 4 5	Adapts the coaching interaction to my needs
1 2 3 4 5	Understands or asks how suggestions and ideas might affect me personally
1 2 3 4 5	Always treats me with respect and dignity
1 2 3 4 5	Is ethical and professional with me
1 2 3 4 5	Always avoids talking down to me or making me feel stupid or inadequate
1 2 3 4 5	Helps me relate my personal goals to organizational goals
1 2 3 4 5	Helps me create realistic goals and timelines for my development
1 2 3 4 5	Gives me the feeling that he/she believes in me and is confident that I will succeed
1 2 3 4 5	Clearly demonstrates skills that guide the interaction and my development
1 2 3 4 5	Is versed in coaching and has my respect
1 2 3 4 5	Always meets commitments regardless of the situation
1 2 3 4 5	Creates an environment of safety and security about sensitive issues
1 2 3 4 5	Establishes and adheres to clear standards regarding our interaction
1 2 3 4 5	Models behavior that I want to emulate
1 2 3 4 5	Does not criticize peers, other clients, or subordinates during our interactions
1 2 3 4 5	Doesn't use jargon or muddled language
1 2 3 4 5	Stands for clear principles and is not afraid to be seen doing so
1 2 3 4 5	Demonstrates persistence while asking me to move forward appropriately
1 2 3 4 5	Focuses on success in the interaction rather than on my failures
1 2 3 4 5	Helps me to constructively view difficult issues

TOTAL SCORE (ADD UP ALL NUMBERS)

SCORING KEY

100	Coaching mismatch
100–150	Average effectiveness
150–200	Above average effectiveness
200	High-performance coaching relationship

Please feel free to relate any positive or negative experiences that you would like to discuss with your coach.

From *The Coaching Starter Kit* by CoachVille.com, published by W. W. Norton & Company, Inc.
Form courtesy of and copyrighted by W. Jan Austin

Coaching Evaluation

My name _____   Date_____

My coach _____

Period evaluated: From ___/___/___ to ___/___/___

Our work has been focused on the following areas: (select as many as apply)

- Increased business productivity and profit
- Health and well-being
- Life planning
- Career development/transition
- Relationship building
- Strategic business planning
- Time/stress/procrastination management
- Special Project: _____
- Other: _____

What have been the key areas of progress during this period? What shifts have taken place that have moved you forward most? _____

_____

Where do we need to do more work in the future? (your major concerns) _____

_____

What are the elements of our relationship that have worked best for you?_____

_____

What continues to frustrate you or hold you back from achieving your goals? _____

_____

How do you feel about the coaching process?

- Excellent—let's continue as we are.
- Good—but I'd like to discuss some changes in how we work.
- Poor—I want to continue but with a different approach.
- Unsatisfied—coaching isn't working for me, I want to stop.

COMMENTS

Use this space to express any concerns, no matter how minor they may seem, that will help your coach to coach you better. This is also a good place to share any new goals or objectives that have occurred to you recently.

_____

_____

_____

_____

From *The Coaching Starter Kit* by CoachVille.com, published by W. W. Norton & Company, Inc.
Form courtesy of and copyrighted by Brian Philcox

275

Client Evaluation of Coach

Please circle the numbers that most represent your response. How well are you being coached?

	NO				YES

HOW VALUABLE WAS / IS YOUR COACHING?

	NO				YES
I am achieving the goals I intended to	1	2	3	4	5
I am achieving additional worthwhile goals	1	2	3	4	5
I now produce results faster/easier because of coaching	1	2	3	4	5
I now have skills from which I will always benefit	1	2	3	4	5

HOW EFFECTIVE IS THE COACH?

The coach is a model for me on how to achieve	1	2	3	4	5
I trust my coach completely	1	2	3	4	5
The coach always treats me with respect	1	2	3	4	5
The coach is rigorous and committed to my success	1	2	3	4	5
The coach is on time and present for all sessions	1	2	3	4	5
The coach is available between calls/sessions	1	2	3	4	5
Within a month of starting, I felt confident in the coach	1	2	3	4	5
I have the paperwork, forms, and worksheets I need	1	2	3	4	5
The coach keeps me focused	1	2	3	4	5

SUMMARY

I will refer clients to the coach	1	2	3	4	5
I receive full value for the fees I pay/paid	1	2	3	4	5
Coaching is successful for me	1	2	3	4	5
The coach is a professional	1	2	3	4	5
The coach is knowledgeable	1	2	3	4	5
The coach brings out my very best	1	2	3	4	5

COMMENTS

_____

_____

_____

_____

_____

_____

From *The Coaching Starter Kit* by CoachVille.com, published by W. W. Norton & Company, Inc.

277

Organizational Leader Coach: 360° Feedback Tool

My coach . . .

COACHING COMPETENCY	RATING	COMMENTS
Creates a safe, supportive environment which encourages exploration of my strengths and limitations, and experimentation with new skills and behaviors		
Expresses confidence in my ability to develop my potential		
Ensures a focus and structure to our coaching sessions		
Listens fully to what I have to say and encourages my truthful self-expression		
Attends to my personal agenda, not his/her agenda for me		
Demonstrates respect for my personal communication and learning style		
Asks questions which demonstrate he/she is actively listening and understands my unique perspective		
Promotes expression of strong emotion without losing his/her objectivity		
Helps me clarify what's important to my success and what constitutes extraordinary performance Uses language which is respectful and free of bias, jargon, or judgment		
Communicates important points or new concepts using personal experience, stories, and concrete examples		
Helps me to identify areas in which my stated intentions and behaviors are not congruent		
Provides support and encouragement when I try new behaviors and actions		

From *The Coaching Starter Kit* by CoachVille.com, published by W. W. Norton & Company, Inc.
Form courtesy of and copyrighted by W. Jan Austin

COACHING COMPETENCY	RATING	COMMENTS
Collaborates on a challenging coaching plan with me that includes specific goals and time frames, and reviews my progress with me on a regular basis		
Celebrates and endorses my successes		
Helps me to see what lies ahead and to identify the learning, experiences, and actions needed to take myself to the next level		
Develops my ability to make decisions, solve problems, and address key concerns		
Offers alternative points of view aligned with my goals, and without attachment or bias, engages me in their consideration		
Demonstrates commitment to high personal and professional standards, and challenges me to raise mine		
Helps me to examine, without judgment or censure, my attitudes, beliefs, and habitual behaviors that do not serve me or my goals		
Makes clear, direct requests for actions, which will move me towards my stated goals		
Supports me when I make mistakes by helping me articulate what's missing from my strategy or where I need to focus		
Helps me to identify and remove obstacles to my success		
Promotes my self-discipline and holds me accountable for my goals and intended actions		
Demonstrates willingness to learn from me; is receptive to my coaching him/her		
Can be counted on to follow through on his/her agreements and commitments in our relationship		

COACHING COMPETENCY	RATING	COMMENTS
Demonstrates commitment to continuous improvement of his/her own skills and capabilities		
Uses humor effectively to create lightness and energy during our coaching sessions		
Is open to a number of ways of working with me; is not locked into a specific technique or formula		
Has a strong professional presence, yet is not afraid to admit when he/she does not know something		

RATING SCALE

1. **Never** engages in the described behavior
2. **Seldom** engages in the described behavior
3. **Usually** engages in the described behavior
4. **Frequently** engages in the described behavior
5. **Always** engages in the described behavior

ADDITIONAL COMMENTS

Form completed for _____   Form completed by_____

Life Coaching Evaluation

Our number one priority is you, our client. It is only through your honest and open feedback that we can continuously improve our services and grow to be the best life coaches we can be. We appreciate you taking the time to complete this evaluation form and return it to us. Please use it as a guide and feel free to add anything you wish. Thank you.

What has been the greatest benefit life coaching has brought you? What outcomes have you achieved? _____
_____

Have any of your initial expectations of the coaching process not been met? If so, what? _____
_____

How effective was your coach? (1 = not very effective, 5 = very effective)

1   5

❏ ❏ ❏ ❏ ❏   My coach was a model for me on how to achieve.

❏ ❏ ❏ ❏ ❏   I trusted my coach, completely.

❏ ❏ ❏ ❏ ❏   My coach always treated me with respect.

❏ ❏ ❏ ❏ ❏   My coach was rigorous and committed to my success.

❏ ❏ ❏ ❏ ❏   My coach was on time and present for all sessions.

❏ ❏ ❏ ❏ ❏   My coach was available between sessions.

❏ ❏ ❏ ❏ ❏   Within a month of starting, I felt confident in my coach.

❏ ❏ ❏ ❏ ❏   My coach kept me focused.

What do you feel your coach's greatest strength is, and how has that supported you? In which areas do you feel your coach could focus their growth? _____
_____

Do you have any comments on the structure of our coaching sessions? (i.e., more or less time, frequency, reviews, paperwork, face-to-face versus telephone) _____
_____

What do you want most from our future partnership, and what would keep this process rewarding? _____
_____

Do you have any other ideas, insights, or suggestions on ways to improve? _____
_____

SUMMARY

1   5

❏ ❏ ❏ ❏ ❏   My coach was able to bring out my very best.

❏ ❏ ❏ ❏ ❏   I received full value for the fees I paid.

❏ ❏ ❏ ❏ ❏   I will refer other people to my coach.

From *The Coaching Starter Kit* by CoachVille.com, published by W. W. Norton & Company, Inc.
Form courtesy of and copyrighted by Thomas Leonard

Chapter 10

Making Progress

SETTING GOALS
10 Keys to Time Management

1. **Start with the recognition that you are not effectively managing your time**
   You can only manage yourself (your attitudes, beliefs, and actions) within the flow of time. The experience of time has more to do with your thoughts than with clock time. The stress you feel that you associate with time originates in your thinking. Effective time management begins with the recognition that our experience of time can improve our attitudes, beliefs, and actions.

2. **Prioritize your efforts**
   Make the distinction between things that are important and things that are urgent. Most of the time, doing the things that are important, rather than urgent, results in greater effectiveness. In other words, don't major in minor things.

3. **Do less to get more**
   Economize your efforts. For example, when you're boiling a pot of water, let it come to a boil while you do something else, or you can "watch the pot."

4. **Reduce excess sources of adrenaline**
   These are substances, activities, relationships, situations, or attitudes that result in your feeling "charged up." Too much adrenaline can distract you from the focus needed to complete a project, increase feelings of anxiety, and intensify the feeling that time is flying. Over time, excessive adrenaline can have negative health consequences as well.

5. **Eliminate time- and energy-taxing elements**
   These are situations, attitudes, or behaviors that you're putting up with in your personal or work life, which don't serve you or your larger purpose but consume physical, mental, and/or emotional energy. Eliminating them results in an increase in available energy for people and projects, an overall feeling of calm, and more time to get things done.

6. **Simplify your environment.**
   Clutter in your office or home environment can create stress. It can actually make you feel like you have more work than you really do.

7. **Simplify your tasks**
   This may involve over-responding and/or under-responding. For example, when receiving a fax, which needs only a quick response or a confirmation, write your answer on the faxed document and fax it right back. Or, if someone asks you for something specific, and you know that by offering more help than was originally asked you can avoid the situation or issue from coming back to you in the form of a problem, then isn't it worth it to do more? Make a point of over-responding to any situation in which there is an opportunity to solve more than one problem in the process.

8. **Really listen to others**
   When you are preoccupied with other thoughts, you actually create anxiety for yourself about what you are listening to and what you allow to intrude into your thoughts. This anxiety is created because you can not act immediately on either. You are left feeling incomplete with both.

9. **Decide what you can give up in order to get what you want**
   One day has only twenty-four hours in it, and yet, how many times have you borrowed from the next day to finish a project thereby losing valuable sleep, or borrowed from your relationships to pursue a goal, or borrowed from your personal time to work on a project? When we choose among multiple possibilities how we will spend our work and/or personal time, we are almost always asked to choose what we will give up in order to have more. Much pain and suffering around "managing time" could be avoided if this process were respected.

10. **Find some time each day for quiet reflection.**
    When you commit to spending some time each day suspending your thoughts and judgments and creating inner stillness, you'll train your body and mind what awareness feels like, and you can transform how you experience the flow of time.

From *The Coaching Starter Kit* by CoachVille.com, published by W. W. Norton & Company, Inc.
Form courtesy of and copyrighted by W. Jan Austin

Resources and Assets

Please respond to each question in the space provided. What do you have going for you?

PERSONAL AND PROFESSIONAL STRENGTHS

Evaluate your strengths and list the top five below.

_____

_____

_____

_____

_____

_____

MOST SIGNIFICANT PERSONAL AND PROFESSIONAL ACCOMPLISHMENTS

What are you most pleased and proud of having accomplished?

_____

_____

_____

_____

_____

_____

PERSONAL AND PROFESSIONAL ASSETS

Who do you know? What do you know? What gifts do you have? What makes you unique and powerful?

_____

_____

_____

_____

_____

THANK YOU.

From *The Coaching Starter Kit* by CoachVille.com, published by W. W. Norton & Company, Inc.

289

Special Project

Use this form to design a project that empowers you.

Project name _____

Specific, measurable result _____

_____

THE PLAN

	START	FINISH	ACTION STEP	MILESTONE / RESULT
1.				
2.				
3.				
4.				
5.				
6.				
7.				
8.				
9.				
10.				
11.				
12.				
13.				
14.				
15.				

Current Status Evaluation

Today's date _____

Name _____ Date of birth _____

Home phone _____ Work phone _____

Fax _____ Pager _____

Cellular _____

E-mail _____ Website _____

Home address _____

City _____ State _____ Zip _____

Work address _____

City _____ State _____ Zip _____

Occupation company _____ Name _____

CHECK THE ITEMS THAT APPLY

❏ Self-employed ❏ Work for someone else ❏ Plan to be self-employed. If so, for how long?

CLASSIFY YOUR OCCUPATION

❏ Professional ❏ Retail ❏ Sales ❏ Service ❏ Home-based ❏ Network Marketing ❏ Other

The purpose of these two exercises is to determine the three things you most want to improve. After you complete the second and third pages of this worksheet, list your three priorities based on your selections in the two exercises.

THREE PRIORITIES

1. _____

2. _____

3. _____

ANALYZE YOUR BUSINESS SKILLS

On the next page are many of the different hats you must wear in order for a business or career to be successful (this is true whether you work for yourself or for someone else; in other words, even if you work for someone else, you have to market yourself, sell your ideas, have a personal vision, etc.). To the right of each category, mark with an "X" where you believe you currently are, and then mark with a star ("★") where you want to be in the next three months. Circle your top three priorities.

From The Coaching Starter Kit by CoachVille.com, published by W. W. Norton & Company, Inc.

293

	NOT SATISFIED	SOMEWHAT SATISFIED	SATISFIED	VERY SATISFIED
Profession (what you do for a living)	❏	❏	❏	❏
Entrepreneur (create and share a compelling vision)	❏	❏	❏	❏
Leadership (eliciting cooperation and participation from others)	❏	❏	❏	❏
Operations (managing processes and day-to-day activities)	❏	❏	❏	❏
Financial (understanding the financial health of business)	❏	❏	❏	❏
Administration	❏	❏	❏	❏
Facilities management (space and equipment)	❏	❏	❏	❏
Human resources (coaching, training, hiring, and firing)	❏	❏	❏	❏
Marketing (meeting people and turning them into prospects)	❏	❏	❏	❏
Sales (turning prospects into customers)	❏	❏	❏	❏
Customer service (keeping promises, following-up)	❏	❏	❏	❏

DETERMINE YOUR LIFESTYLE TRAITS

Put a mark in the part of the spectrum where you think you are, relative to the choices on each side. When you are done with each section, pick the top three overall traits you want to improve. Mark them on the right as a 1, 2, or 3, with "1" being your highest priority. When you finish this page and the next, go back to the front of the form and list your top three overall priorities.

Business Development
Priority

Don't have/share compelling vision with others	❏ ❏ ❏ ❏ ❏ Have and share compelling vision with others	_____
Don't know all business functions	❏ ❏ ❏ ❏ ❏ Take responsibility for all business functions	_____
Don't know the sales cycle	❏ ❏ ❏ ❏ ❏ Use the sales cycle effectively	_____
Don't know how to manage cash flow	❏ ❏ ❏ ❏ ❏ Manage cash flow, follow budget (with savings)	_____
Don't have a niche or specialty	❏ ❏ ❏ ❏ ❏ Am known as an expert in a specialty	_____
Over-promise and under-deliver	❏ ❏ ❏ ❏ ❏ Under-promise and over-deliver	_____
Have few referrals from clients and networks	❏ ❏ ❏ ❏ ❏ Have many referrals, wide client base	_____
Provide poor quality goods and services	❏ ❏ ❏ ❏ ❏ Customers are delighted with my goods and services	_____
Business is stagnant	❏ ❏ ❏ ❏ ❏ Business is expanding	_____

From The Coaching Starter Kit by CoachVille.com, published by W. W. Norton & Company, Inc.

Professional Development   **Priority**

Career/profession not aligned with values	❑ ❑ ❑ ❑	Career/profession chosen due to my life's values	_____
Am not master/expert of trade/profession	❑ ❑ ❑ ❑	Master and expert of my trade/profession	_____
Lack tools/equipment/knowledge to succeed	❑ ❑ ❑ ❑	Have and use tools/equipment/knowledge	_____
Don't manage projects or processes well	❑ ❑ ❑ ❑	Successful at managing projects and processes	_____
Can't overcome objections and close sales	❑ ❑ ❑ ❑	Successfully overcome objections/close sales	_____
Poor communication (speaking, listening, writing)	❑ ❑ ❑ ❑	Excellent communication skills	_____
Only working in business (performing daily tasks)	❑ ❑ ❑ ❑	Spend time working on business (visions, plans)	_____
Don't complete tasks, projects, goals	❑ ❑ ❑ ❑	Complete tasks, projects, goals	_____
Become defensive when faced with feedback	❑ ❑ ❑ ❑	View feedback as a way to learn and improve	_____

Personal Development   **Priority**

Don't know who I am or where I'm going	❑ ❑ ❑ ❑	Have clearly defined vision, values, mission/purpose	_____
Dissatisfied with relationships with others	❑ ❑ ❑ ❑	Satisfied with relationships with others	_____
Dislike appearance, health, and fitness level	❑ ❑ ❑ ❑	Satisfied with appearance, health, fitness level	_____
Unfulfilling, stagnant, unbalanced lifestyle	❑ ❑ ❑ ❑	Fulfilling, dynamic, balanced lifestyle	_____
Lack of motivation, enthusiasm, energy	❑ ❑ ❑ ❑	Motivated, enthusiastic, energetic	_____
Possess negative self-image, question self-worth	❑ ❑ ❑ ❑	Possess positive self-image, confidence in self-worth	_____
High stress level, don't manage stress well	❑ ❑ ❑ ❑	Low stress level, manage stress well, can relax	_____
Feel hurried, rushed, pressured, often late	❑ ❑ ❑ ❑	Calmly and easily manage time, early or on time	_____
Don't know what I need or how to satisfy needs	❑ ❑ ❑ ❑	Am assertive in order to satisfy my needs	_____

Process/Project Management   **Priority**

Don't have vision of desired outcome	❑ ❑ ❑ ❑	Clearly defined vision of desired outcome	_____
Don't set specific, measurable goals	❑ ❑ ❑ ❑	Goals are specific, measurable, and in writing	_____
Unable to develop achievable action plans	❑ ❑ ❑ ❑	Able to develop achievable action plans	_____
Take on all responsibilities, do all the work	❑ ❑ ❑ ❑	Delegate responsibility, motivate others to action	_____
Unable to see roadblocks, obstacles, delays	❑ ❑ ❑ ❑	Foresee and plan for roadblocks, delays	_____
Don't identify needed resources	❑ ❑ ❑ ❑	Know how to and do identify needed resources	_____
Don't manage resources well	❑ ❑ ❑ ❑	Know how to and manage resources well	_____
Don't measure progress	❑ ❑ ❑ ❑	Know how to and measure progress	_____
Stick to original plans no matter what	❑ ❑ ❑ ❑	Can adjust to circumstances as they arise	_____
Don't evaluate results, return on investment	❑ ❑ ❑ ❑	Can and do evaluate results	_____
Can't identify lessons learned	❑ ❑ ❑ ❑	Identify/Use new awarenesses, lessons learned	_____
Don't recognize, reward, celebrate successes	❑ ❑ ❑ ❑	Recognize, reward, celebrate wins/successes	_____

Well-Formed Outcome: Criteria by Which to Evaluate Your Goals

Name_____ Date_____

1. **State your goal in positive terms.** Describe the outcome in terms of what you want rather than what you don't want. What specifically do you want?

_____

_____

2. **Can you initiate and maintain your goal?** Is achieving the outcome within your control?   ❏ Yes ❏ No

   If achieving the outcome is within your control, go for it. If not, either redesign it so it is, or let go of it. You can only control yourself, and that's challenging enough.

3. **Describe your outcome in sensory-based words.** How will you know when you have reached your desired outcome? What will you see, hear, and feel when you have it?

_____

_____

4. **Is your goal testable and measurable?** By what date will you achieve your desired outcome?
   - What will you be measuring?_____
   - What is your starting point? _____
   - Desired goal? _____

5. **Congruency.** Is your desired outcome aligned with your highest good?   ❏ Yes ❏ No

   Is it aligned with who you are and what's important to you?   ❏ Yes ❏ No

   Does it create/contribute to a win-win situation for all involved?   ❏ Yes ❏ No

   Proceed if you answered "yes" to all three questions. If not, closely examine what you want and why.

   Is your desired outcome SMART?
   - **Specific:** Identify exactly what you want. Describe the outcome in detail.
   - **Measurable:** Quantify your outcomes—how much, how big, how long, etc.
   - **Active:** Plan your work; work your plan. Actively prioritize the many tasks at hand.
   - **Realistic:** You can accomplish the outcome if you make a reasonable stretch.
   - **Time-Targeted:** Designate a target date for completion.

_____

Now make a powerful, concise statement of your SMART, well-formed desired outcome!

_____

_____

ADDITIONAL CRITERIA TO EXPLORE AS YOU DEVELOP YOUR GOALS AND PLANS

1. **What is the result of getting this outcome?** What will happen if you get what you want?

_____

_____

How will getting the outcome affect your life?

_____

_____

What will you gain if you achieve your outcome?

_____

_____

What becomes possible if you achieve it?

_____

_____

What won't happen if you achieve it? What will happen if you don't achieve it?

_____

_____

Does the outcome increase the choices available to you?	Yes	No
Does achieving the outcome support you?	Yes	No
Does achieving the outcome add value to you and your life?	Yes	No
Does achieving the outcome add value to those impacted by the outcome?	Yes	No
Does achieving the outcome add value to those for whom there is an indirect impact?	Yes	No

2. **In what context is the outcome preferable?** Where, when, how, and with whom do you ideally want it?

_____

_____

_____

_____

From _The Coaching Starter Kit_ by CoachVille.com, published by W. W. Norton & Company, Inc.
Form courtesy of and copyrighted by Bonnie Dubrow, Strategies for Success, Inc.

3. **How do you know the outcome is worth getting?** This may be the most important criteria of all.

_____

_____

_____

_____

When you are actively involved in tasks required to achieve the outcome
 or when you think about achieving it, are you excited?   Yes   No

Are you passionate about doing what's necessary?   Yes   No

Are you passionate about the desired results?   Yes   No

Do you get to share your gifts?   Yes   No

Do you experience joy while you are achieving the outcome?   Yes   No

If the answers to these questions are "yes," chances are the outcome is worth getting.

4. **Create many ways to get the outcome.** Generate at least three options so you can have options.

_____

_____

_____

_____

_____

5. **What resources are needed?**

RESOURCES	HAVE	NEED	RESOURCES	HAVE	NEED

From _The Coaching Starter Kit_ by CoachVille.com, published by W. W. Norton & Company, Inc.
Form courtesy of and copyrighted by Bonnie Dubrow, Strategies for Success, Inc.

What resources do you already have? On the previous page, put a check under the column labeled "Have."

Which ones will you need to obtain? Put a check under the column labeled "Get."

Have you ever achieved your desired outcome before?   Yes No

Do you know anyone who has?   Yes No

You might want to talk to them, read books about them, do what you can to learn from them.

6. **First steps towards a goal should be specific and achievable.** Make a list of the steps that have already come to mind and prioritize them. Then take action. As you do, new steps and new possibilities will become apparent.

_____

_____

_____

_____

_____

Make a habit of exploring each outcome or goal in terms of these criteria. You will become competent and confident in your ability to create and choose outcomes that inspire and motivate you.

Once you have developed a well-formed outcome, visualize yourself having already achieved it. Create an affirmation and repeat it often, at least twice daily, with powerful, positive feelings. Doing so will keep you excited, on task, and help attract the outcome to you (whether you believe it or not).

From *The Coaching Starter Kit* by CoachVille.com, published by W. W. Norton & Company, Inc.
Form courtesy of and copyrighted by Bonnie Dubrow, Strategies for Success, Inc.

OVERCOMING OBSTACLES
Anger Is Energy

Questions to consider when you are angry.

1. What am I angry about?

   _____

   _____

2. Are my feelings in proportion to the event that triggered my anger?

   _____

   _____

3. If they are not, you may be experiencing archaic anger, or anger that has roots in the past. To clarify, answer these questions

   When have I felt this way before?

   _____

   _____

   What did I do about the feeling then?

   _____

   _____

4. What is the problem to be solved?

   _____

   _____

5. What is the outcome I want to achieve?

   _____

   _____

6. Is the goal worth achieving?

   _____

   _____

7. What are the action steps I need to take to achieve my goal?

   _____

   _____

From *The Coaching Starter Kit* by CoachVille.com, published by W. W. Norton & Company, Inc.
Form courtesy of and copyrighted by Laurie Weiss, Ph.D.

What to Do About Fear

When you feel scared, nervous, anxious, etc., answer these questions.

1. Is there something happening or going to happen that is dangerous? If so, what is the danger? Is it real or imagined? If there is no danger, is there something I am excited about? (The physical sensations of fear and excitement are very similar.)

_____

_____

_____

_____

_____

2. How likely is it that the danger will cause me harm?

_____

_____

_____

_____

_____

3. Is there anything I can do to protect myself?

_____

_____

_____

_____

_____

4. If the very worst thing I can imagine happens, what will I do?

_____

_____

_____

_____

_____

From *The Coaching Starter Kit* by CoachVille.com, published by W. W. Norton & Company, Inc.
Form courtesy of and copyrighted by Laurie Weiss, Ph.D.

Possibility

- If you had all the money you needed, where and how would you live?

- If you had the answers to your problems, how long would it take to solve them?

- Do you have a personal or professional vision? If so, what is it?

- What is probably not possible for you to achieve in this lifetime that you wish you could?

- On a scale of 1 to 10, with ten being the highest, how would you rate the quality of your life today?

- Using that same scale, how high will that number likely rise during your lifetime?

- What is a dream or goal on which you've given up?

- What part of *you* have you given up on?

- What goal or part of your life have you put on the back burner because the time isn't right? What part of you is just waiting for the right person or opportunity to catalyze it?

From *The Coaching Starter Kit* by CoachVille.com, published by W. W. Norton & Company, Inc.

The Extraordinary Wonder of Obstacles

Have you made up your mind that you are going to achieve the things you want out of life no matter what obstacles you come up against? What would your responses have been like in the past? Take the time to think about the times that you did give up. Think back to several goals or dreams you had in the past. Mentally relive the experience that led up to your quitting the pursuit of your goal.

When you can remember at least three times in your life when you stopped short of achieving what you had planned, list them in the first column on the chart below. In the second column, write down what it was that stopped you from pursuing your dream or goal. Identify the obstacle that came into your path. Document specifically what it was that caused you to give up on this dream.

Then, write down what you could have done to achieve your goal. Was there some action that you could have taken to overcome the obstacles that challenged you at that time? Write down everything that comes to mind in the third column.

By completing this exercise, many people realize that they were very close to achieving their dream when they quit trying because of one obstacle or another. Ask yourself, what you can do now to recapture the desire to achieve your dream and renew your passion.

WHAT I WANTED	WHY I GAVE UP	WHAT I COULD HAVE DONE

5 Sources of the Most Common Problems That People Have

You can spend hours trying to explain/sell coaching to prospective clients, or you can simply sell a solution to the problems your potential clients are having. People do not usually buy coaching per se; they buy solutions provided by someone they trust. And along that line, knowing the top sources to the problems that most people seem to have will allow you to orient your coaching around solutions.

PROBLEM 1. PEOPLE SEEK HAPPINESS FROM EXTERNAL SOURCES

I call these the "brand chasers," "strivers," or the "if/then'ers." They are under the impression that if they do enough, have enough, or become enough, they will be happy. This ends up being an endless cycle of action, movement, and effort, yet the person does not wake up happy or go to bed happy. For these individuals, life is lived in the future by mortgaging the present.

PROBLEM 2. PEOPLE DO NOT HAVE ENOUGH OF WHAT THEY REALLY NEED

Clutter and tolerations seem to be the most obvious symptoms of those who are behind in terms of managing their lives. And the source is that they do not have enough of what they need—information, support, love, money, space, reserves, etc. Life has become so demanding and complex, and we have simply not kept up with the emotional and structural development we need to stay ahead of this train called life.

PROBLEM 3. PEOPLE OFTEN SEE THEMSELVES AS A PLANET, INSTEAD OF THE SUN

American culture has always been about the individual, the pioneer, the innovator—not the group or society. Good or bad, we do not have the familial, social, or cultural tethers that those in other cultures do. As everyone becomes connected via the Internet, the old paradigm of group versus individual is much less relevant. What matters is that you have something to offer the world around you. One of the fastest ways to understand this is to start looking at yourself as the sun versus being a lonely planet. It's a huge step for many, but an essential evolutionary step for all.

PROBLEM 4. PEOPLE ARE OPERATING ON OLD MEMES AND ASSUMPTIONS

Memes (ideas, concepts, principles) are evolving at a rate faster than society's ability to digest, integrate, assimilate, and reorient around them. Conduits such as institutions, corporations, churches, and governments have traditionally been used to accept and evolve itself. Given the mounting pressure building from a backlog of unaccepted new ideas, new conduits are being created as workarounds to relieve the pressure. Thus, the Internet and self-organizing virtual networks have become possible. Part of what a coach does is to help clients update their collection of memes.

PROBLEM 5. PEOPLE DON'T LIVE IN SUFFICIENTLY STIMULATING ENVIRONMENTS

Most people do not receive enough intellectual, creative, emotional, or spiritual stimulation from their environments. This is because they are either in a job that does not challenge/evolve them, or they watch too much TV, or they are in a sleepy relationship, and they do not have any room for new sources of stimulation. The solution is to show the client how to become a master crafter of all of their environments—physical, personal, emotional, and spiritual. When properly designed, environments do all of the work and effort in a person's life, and filter out most of the bad habits, distractions, and diversions.

From *The Coaching Starter Kit* by CoachVille.com, published by W. W. Norton & Company, Inc.
Form courtesy of and copyrighted by Thomas Leonard

TAKING ACTION
Life Purpose Worksheet

Why are you alive?

What are you most proud of having accomplished at this point in your life? _____

_____

_____

If you were financially able to retire one year from today, what would you begin working on to prepare for that?

_____

_____

What would you most like the people at your funeral to say about you, specifically? _____

_____

_____

Who in history do you admire most and why? _____

_____

_____

If you could solve a world problem, what would it be? Be very specific please. _____

_____

_____

What is in the way of putting this ahead of what you are engaged in now? _____

_____

_____

If it weren't important to have a life purpose, what would you most like to do in the next decade? _____

_____

_____

List three possible life purposes: _____

_____

_____

From *The Coaching Starter Kit* by CoachVille.com, published by W. W. Norton & Company, Inc.

Uncovering the Fundamental Lie

The fundamental lie is that false assumption, life misunderstanding, or stale formula which dictates many of our thoughts, actions, and results. The fundamental lie is the kind of thing that takes a knock on the side of the head to see and tell the truth about. Use the space below to tell the truth about your fundamental lie:

What is true about your parents that you've never been able to see/articulate until now?

_____

_____

_____

What is true about the failures you've had in life? Who was to blame? _____

_____

_____

_____

What do you say that you are ready for, but have not had significant results in or progress towards in the last two years?_____

_____

_____

What childish fantasies are you still subjecting yourself to? _____

_____

_____

What are you holding onto hope about? _____

_____

_____

What's the secret you are most concerned about people discovering? _____

_____

_____

List three possible fundamental lies. _____

_____

_____

What is the next step?_____

_____

_____

_____

From *The Coaching Starter Kit* by CoachVille.com, published by W. W. Norton & Company, Inc.

315

Priorities

Most clients appreciate support to identify and focus on the most important goals.

- What is your most urgent personal problem?

- What is your most urgent business problem?

- What problems feel unsolvable right now?

- What are the three biggest changes you wish to make in your life over the next ninety days?

- What are the three biggest changes you will need to make in your life over the next three years?

- What are the three biggest opportunities you have right now that you are not making the most of?

- What feeling is most important for you to have a lot more of, and quickly?

- What goal/outcome do you have that you are pining for or are really ready to achieve?

- What is the single focus for our coaching that will help you reach multiple goals?

- What is pressing most on your mind today that you are willing to share with me?

From *The Coaching Starter Kit* by CoachVille.com, published by W. W. Norton & Company, Inc.

317

Action Plan

Complete the following action plan.

Originator: _____   Date: _____

Distribution: _____   Page _____ of _____

Specific Objective: _____

_____

_____

_____

ACTION STEPS	RESPONSIBILITY	DUE DATE	COMPLETION DATE

The Action Log

This is a tool for recording and tracking action items. It clarifies what is to be done, provides regular review of actions, and a traceable record of actual completion.

ACTION LOG

Name: _____

Meeting Date: _____ Page _____ of _____

ITEM #	TASK TO BE COMPLETED	PERSON RESPONSIBLE	TODAY'S DATE	ESTIMATED COMPLETION DATE	WHAT ACTION/S WILL COMPLETE THIS ITEM?	COMMENTS

From *The Coaching Starter Kit* by CoachVille.com, published by W. W. Norton & Company, Inc.
Form courtesy of and copyrighted by Kate Arendt, Genesis Consulting and Coaching

321

Chapter 11

Target Issues

FINANCIAL CONCERNS
Money

Almost all coaching has a financial aspect to it.

- How is your financial situation?

- How stable is your income stream?

- Do you live within, at, or beyond your means?

- Are you a natural saver or a habitual spender?

- How much credit card debt are you carrying?

- How much money is enough for you?

- What actions could you take that would double your current salary? Profit?

- What mistakes do you seem to make with money?

- How much of a priority is making more money?

- What holds you back financially?

From *The Coaching Starter Kit* by CoachVille.com, published by W.W. Norton & Company, Inc.

325

Money Interview Questions

Read and understand the questions below, then follow the directions.

When getting a better understanding of your relationship with money, it is vital that you see where your ideas come from. The easiest way to do this is by interviewing your past.

Review each area below and interview the people indicated. Do not make anyone or any system wrong, just learn.

THE PAST

Parents

What were the rules?

What did they believe in?

How did they impart their wisdom to you?

Siblings

What were the rules?

What did they believe in?

How did they impart their wisdom to you?

School/education

What were the rules?

What did they believe in?

How did they impart their wisdom to you?

Work/career

What were the rules?

What did they believe in?

How did they impart their wisdom to you?

Your Spouse

What were the rules?

What did they believe in?

How did they impart their wisdom to you?

Your Past

What was your worst money decision?

What was the best?

What decisions did you make?

THE PRESENT

What are the gaps in your money "life"?

How are you spending your money?

Where do you want to grow?

THE FUTURE

What will you need to live comfortably?

How much surplus do you want?

From *The Coaching Starter Kit* by CoachVille.com, published by W. W. Norton & Company, Inc.
Form courtesy of and copyrighted by Kenneth Abrams

Annual Spending Plan

Complete the chart.

LIVING	JAN	FEB	MAR	APRIL	MAY	JUNE	JULY	AUG	SEPT	OCT	NOV	DEC
Mortgage/rent												
Electric												
Gas												
Water/sewer												
Telephone												
Cable												
Groceries												
Auto payment												
Auto fuel												
Auto service												
Clothing												
Household												
INSURANCE												
Auto												
Home												
Legal												

From *The Coaching Starter Kit* by CoachVille.com, published by W. W. Norton & Company, Inc.

ENTERTAINMENT	JAN	FEB	MAR	APRIL	MAY	JUNE	JULY	AUG	SEPT	OCT	NOV	DEC
Dining												
Hobbies												
Movies												
Vacation												
DEBTS (CREDIT CARDS, LOANS, ETC.)												
SAVINGS												
TOTAL												

From *The Coaching Starter Kit* by CoachVille.com, published by W. W. Norton & Company, Inc.

Income Date Spending Plan

Complete the chart.

INCOME DATE												
INCOME AMOUNT $												
LIVING												
Mortgage/rent												
Electric												
Gas												
Water/sewer							'					
Telephone												
Cable												
Groceries												
Auto payment												
Auto fuel												
Auto service												
Clothing												
Household												
INSURANCE												
Auto												
Home												
Legal												

From *The Coaching Starter Kit* by CoachVille.com, published by W. W. Norton & Company, Inc.

ENTERTAINMENT											
Dining											
Hobbies											
Movies											
Vacation											
DEBTS (CREDIT CARDS, LOANS, ETC.)											
SAVINGS											
TOTAL SPENDING											

From *The Coaching Starter Kit* by CoachVille.com, published by W. W. Norton & Company, Inc.

Spending / Debt Questionnaire

Circle the number that comes closest to representing how true the statement is for you right now. Then score yourself, using the key at the bottom of the page.

LESS TRUE		MORE TRUE			STATEMENT
1	2	3	4	5	This month's bills come in before I have paid last month's bills.
1	2	3	4	5	I receive at least one cutoff/past due notice per month.
1	2	3	4	5	I have a stack of unopened bills/notices.
1	2	3	4	5	I keep a negative running balance in my checkbook.
1	2	3	4	5	I search for products I can buy with minimal down payments.
1	2	3	4	5	I get excited about how much credit line I have left.
1	2	3	4	5	I get at least one cash advance per month from my credit card.
1	2	3	4	5	I am frequently short a few dollars and borrow from friends, etc.
1	2	3	4	5	I get a high from telling the clerk to "charge it."
1	2	3	4	5	I am always interested in getting new charge cards.
1	2	3	4	5	I feel inordinately good when I pay routine bills like the phone or the rent.
1	2	3	4	5	I am reticent about discussions of money and walk away from social conversations about it.
1	2	3	4	5	I have had an account closed in the last six months and am angry about it or have blamed others.
1	2	3	4	5	When my paycheck or loan money comes in, I experience a great sense of relief.
1	2	3	4	5	I rarely keep a running balance in my checkbook.
1	2	3	4	5	My credit card balances run near the maximum credit line.
1	2	3	4	5	I have little or no savings, investments, or assets; nothing available for contingencies.
1	2	3	4	5	I bounce more than three checks per year.
1	2	3	4	5	I have only a vague idea of my various financial obligations.
1	2	3	4	5	Money is tight, but there is always someone I keep turning to who won't let me starve.

TOTAL SCORE (ADD UP ALL NUMBERS)

SCORING KEY

20–35	Doesn't look like a problem
36–50	Get on a budget!
51–75	Borderline situation
76–100	Clearly a problem

From *The Coaching Starter Kit* by CoachVille.com, published by W. W. Norton & Company, Inc.

Personal Budget: 1-Year Plan

INCOME	JAN	FEB	MAR	APR	MAY	JUNE	JULY	AUGUST	SEPT	OCT	NOV	DEC
Paycheck total												
Commissions												
Business profit												
Investments												
Other income												

TOTAL INCOME

EXPENSES

Auto gas/service												
Auto payments												
Auto insurance												
Bank charges												
Charity												
Child care												
Clothing												
Dining out												
Education												
Entertainment												
Gifts												
Groceries												
Home												
Insurance												
Home												

From *The Coaching Starter Kit* by CoachVille.com, published by W. W. Norton & Company, Inc.

335

	JAN	FEB	MAR	APR	MAY	JUNE	JULY	AUGUST	SEPT	OCT	NOV	DEC
Payments												
Home repair												
Home taxes												
Home utilities												
Household items												
Interest expense												
Investment expenses												
Medical expenses/insurance												
Miscellaneous												
Taxes (income/SS)												
Telephone												
TOTAL EXPENSE												

WHAT'S LEFT?

USES FOR IT

From *The Coaching Starter Kit* by CoachVille.com, published by W. W. Norton & Company, Inc.

Personal Budget: 5-Year Plan

INCOME	200_	200_	200_	200_	200_	200_	TOTAL
Paycheck total							
Commissions							
Business profit							
Investments							
Other income							
TOTAL INCOME							

EXPENSES							
Auto gas/service							
Auto payments							
Auto insurance							
Bank charges							
Charity							
Child care							
Clothing							
Dining out							
Education							
Entertainment							
Gifts							
Groceries							
Home							
Insurance							
Home							

	200_	200_	200_	200_	200_	200_	TOTAL
Payments							
Home repair							
Home taxes							
Home utilities							
Household items							
Interest expense							
Investment expenses							
Medical expenses/insurance							
Miscellaneous							
Taxes (income/SS)							
Telephone							
TOTAL EXPENSE							

WHAT'S LEFT?

USES FOR IT

From *The Coaching Starter Kit* by CoachVille.com, published by W. W. Norton & Company, Inc.

Debt Pay-Off Schedule

7-month form.

SOURCE OF DEBT	DEBT 1	DEBT 2	DEBT 3	DEBT 4	DEBT 5	DEBT 6	DEBT 7	DEBT 8
Month of								
$ Due								
− Payment								
+ Interest								
= Remaining								
Month of								
$ Due								
− Payment								
+ Interest								
= Remaining								
Month of								
$ Due								
− Payment								
+ Interest								
= Remaining								
Month of								
$ Due								
− Payment								
+ Interest								
= Remaining								

From *The Coaching Starter Kit* by CoachVille.com, published by W.W. Norton & Company, Inc.

339

SOURCE OF DEBT	DEBT 1	DEBT 2	DEBT 3	DEBT 4	DEBT 5	DEBT 6	DEBT 7	DEBT 8
Month of								
$ Due								
− Payment								
+ Interest								
= Remaining								
Month of								
$ Due								
− Payment								
+ Interest								
= Remaining								
Month of								
$ Due								
− Payment								
+ Interest								
= Remaining								
Month of								
$ Due								
− Payment								
+ Interest								
= Remaining								

New Money Questionnaire

Read the questions for insight into your personal finances.

1. Do you enjoy your work?

2. Do you visualize yourself achieving something bigger than what you are currently doing?

3. Do you save money every month?

4. Do you invest at least some of your money directly in the stock market either through mutual funds, 401(k), or individual stocks?

5. Do you shop around before you buy most items, especially big-ticket items?

6. Do you take care of your home or apartment, performing regular maintenance, as well as repairs?

7. Do you perform regular maintenance on your car and other expensive items?

8. Do you pay off your credit cards each month?

9. Are you comfortable buying used big-ticket items such as cars and appliances?

10. Do you have insurance protection for your family members and/or business?

11. Have you ever estimated how much money you would need to cover your current expenses?

12. Do you measure the performance results of your portfolio at least yearly?

13. Do you maximize contributions to retirement plans such as 401(k) or IRA?

14. Is your mortgage/rent payment more than 20 percent of your monthly income?

15. Do you spend less than you make?

16. Have you ever read books on building wealth, or an autobiography of someone who is wealthy?

17. Do you own a business now that produces a positive net income?

18. Do you pay your taxes on time every year?

From *The Coaching Starter Kit* by CoachVille.com, published by W. W. Norton & Company, Inc.

CAREER CONCERNS
First Steps to Setting Career Goals

We all have dreams. However, most of the time we spend thinking about our dreams we seem to find reasons not to pursue them. The following questions are a preliminary step in discovering what your dreams are, who you are, and how you feel towards change.

On a piece of paper, respond to the following questions. As you answer these questions, you may have more of your own that come up, just write them down and answer them, too. You will want to use a separate sheet for each of your dreams so they do not get mixed up. These questions are to weigh the pros and cons of your dreams as you see them. You can then take the answers to your personal coach to brainstorm and discover the best way you can achieve your goals, find solutions to your concerns and fears, and turn your dream into a reality.

1. What is your dream?

2. Is your dream feasible? (Can it become a career or is it just for fun?)

3. Do you have any problems (such as medical or physical) that would make pursuing this dream infeasible? (i.e. you always dreamed of being a pilot but your eyesight is beginning to fail you—in all probability this dream would not be achievable.)

4. Does following this dream require a lot of education, time, and money in order to achieve it?

5. Do you have any skills that are transferrable to your dream job?

6. Are you financially capable of pursuing the dream, whether you have a savings account, need a student loan, a personal loan, etc.?

7. If you are unable to quit your current job, can this dream be achieved on a part-time basis? (i.e., night classes, working a second job, etc.)

8. What do you find so ideal about this dream?

9. What does that tell you about yourself?

10. How would you feel if you could turn your dream into reality?

11. Do you automatically find anything negative about this dream? If so, what?

12. Does anything about this dream scare you?

13. Do you feel you are up to the challenge?

14. Do you have support from others in pursuing a change in your career?

15. How difficult was it for you to answer these questions? Or, how easy?

From *The Coaching Starter Kit* by CoachVille.com, published by W. W. Norton & Company, Inc.

Career Assessment

Help the client perfect their work or working environment.

- What are the five things you spend most of your time doing during your workday?

- How much more money could you be making if you focused and were properly inspired and supported?

- Where is the stress coming from in your work?

- Are you working with the right/best people?

- What conflicts are you having at work?

- What is the most fulfilling aspect of your work?

- What is the most difficult or stressful part of your work?

- What is the most exciting aspect of your work?

- What strengths/skills do you have that are immediately marketable?

- What resources are missing that you feel are necessary for your success?

From *The Coaching Starter Kit* by CoachVille.com, published by W.W. Norton & Company, Inc.

345

Your Ideal Job Exercise

Take an entire week to complete the following exercise. The goal is to visualize your ideal job and determine what you want and do not want in your next career position. The process will assist you in creating a career commitment plan. Complete the chart on the next page, using the following nine steps.

STEP 1

In the first column, answer the following question:

What do you have in this job or that you had in past jobs that you do not want in your next career position (work tasks, environment, types of people, etc.)?

STEP 2

In the second column, answer the following question:

What do you have in this job, or had in past jobs, that you do want in your next career position.

STEP 3

In the third column, answer the following question:

What have you not had in a job that you want as part of your next career position?

STEP 4

During the week, add or delete items in the three columns.

STEP 5

Highlight those items in each column that speak to you most.

STEP 6

When preparing your goals, do not set any goals related to column one.

STEP 7

Do include in your commitment plan those things that must be included in your next career position.

STEP 8

Identify those items you will need to develop in column three by placing a (–) beside them. These activities can become part of your commitment plan.

STEP 9

Commit five items that are non-negotiables in any position. Place a (+) next to these items.

From *The Coaching Starter Kit* by CoachVille.com, published by W. W. Norton & Company, Inc.

347

COLUMN ONE	COLUMN TWO	COLUMN THREE
What are the things you have in this job or had in past jobs, that you do not want as part of your next job?	*What are the things you have in this job or had in past jobs, that you do want as part of your next job?*	*What have you not yet had in a job that you want as part of your next job?*